MYRTLEFIELD

HOUSE

Journeys
with Jesus

Journeys
with Jesus

True Stories of Changed
Destinies in John's Gospel

David Gooding

EDITED BY JOSHUA FITZHUGH

Myrtlefield Discoveries

Journeys with Jesus: True Stories of Changed Destinies in John's Gospel

Cover design, interior design and composition: Matthew Craig

First published, 2021
Published by The Myrtlefield Trust
PO BOX 2216
Belfast
N Ireland
BT1 9YR

w: www.myrtlefieldhouse.com
e: info@myrtlefieldhouse.com

ISBN: 978-1-912721-66-5 (hbk.)
ISBN: 978-1-912721-67-2 (pbk.)
ISBN: 978-1-912721-68-9 (PDF)
ISBN: 978-1-912721-69-6 (Kindle)
ISBN: 978-1-912721-70-2 (EPUB without DRM)

25 24 23 22 21   10 9 8 7 6 5 4 3 2 1

Contents

Publisher's Preface

Among all the varied gifts that helped David Gooding communicate God's word effectively, his ability as a storyteller was one of the most compelling. He is known by some for his academic work in the Greek translation of the Hebrew Old Testament, the Septuagint. By many Bible students, he is known for his ability to show how Scripture has been carefully written: its authors selecting and arranging their record of historical events in such a way as to bring out the intention of the Holy Spirit who was guiding them. Many more know him as a preacher, whether they heard him in person or by listening to recordings of a ministry that spanned many decades.

No one who ever heard Dr Gooding preach will be likely to overlook his ability to retell the stories of the Bible. He could lead you into a narrative until you felt you were there as the event happened: whether it was Peter as he felt himself sinking beneath the waves, or Moses standing between the people and the righteous indignation of God on Sinai, or the aged Abraham and Sarah as they sat together at the campfire trying to decide how they could help God fulfil his promise to them. He enlisted his audience's imagination as an ally in the work of understanding God's revelation of himself in the pages of Scripture.

Journeys with Jesus has been prepared with the same aim in mind. Its chapters have been compiled from Dr Gooding's published sermon transcripts and books, and unpublished manuscripts on John's Gospel. The touchstone for each selection has been that it teaches mainly through telling the story that John has recorded. Some provoke the reader's imagination more than others; some speculate about details that are not explicitly stated in the account; but all are subject to the text and direct us to engage with the events that are unfolding before our eyes.

This criterion also helps to explain why certain key stories from John's Gospel are not included. There is no chapter dedicated to the feeding of the five thousand, for instance, nor to the woman caught in adultery in John 8, or to the healing of the blind man in John 9. Dr Gooding did teach on those portions, but not always in the same style that we find here when he takes us along on Nathanael's journey of faith, or into the conversation with the woman at the well. Anyone who would like a more comprehensive book on his teaching on the whole of John's Gospel need not despair, because we are currently preparing just such a book for publication. In the meantime, a listing of his sermons and other resources on John's Gospel, which can be freely downloaded, can be found at the end of this book.

Among those who have contributed their own gifts to this project, two people should be especially mentioned. Through the years of assisting Dr Gooding in his ministry, and in the work of carefully transcribing and editing his sermons, Mrs Barbara Hamilton has, quite literally, made this book possible. Likewise, it would not exist but for the quiet encouragement and behind the scenes service of Prof. Arthur Williamson who has long insisted that the archive from which these chapters are drawn should be prepared, preserved and published to the world. This is, as he has so often said, a day of good tidings; so let us not remain silent. And it is the prayer of everyone at Myrtlefield House that many will hear the voice of God speaking his living word directly to them, so that they may begin, or else continue with a deeper faith, their journey with the Lord Jesus.

Joshua Fitzhugh
Belfast, 2021

Introduction

The New Testament is a book of wonderful variety. It contains profound theological treatises and mysterious apocalyptic visions along with straightforward historical narrative. But perhaps the feature that endears it most to people is the frequent pen-sketches it contains of individual men and women who lived in the time of our Lord.

Few of these sketches are very long, and some of the people they describe are only mentioned once in the whole of the New Testament. And yet the records are so vivid that we feel we know the persons they are talking about. We sense their temperaments, we feel their problems, we understand their spiritual difficulties as though they were our next door neighbours or friends.

In these studies in the Gospel of John we shall be tracing the spiritual pilgrimages of some of these people, studying their background, diagnosing their problems, watching their reactions on first meeting Jesus Christ, and following the steps by which many of them eventually came to personal faith in him and to the experience of salvation. Along the way, we will pause occasionally to be sure that we are hearing what this Gospel has to say to us.

After all, John's Gospel is about conversion to Christ, and we have missed its point if we do not soon become aware that it is not meant simply to entertain us as literature, or stimulate us with intellectual exercises, but is also intended to lead us personally to faith in Christ. And it may well help us, either as we come to him or as we grow to know him better, if we think imaginatively through the processes by which other people came to Christ, and believed.

From Prejudice *to* Faith

The next day Jesus decided to go to Galilee. He found Philip and said to him, 'Follow me.'

Now Philip was from Bethsaida, the city of Andrew and Peter. Philip found Nathanael and said to him, 'We have found him of whom Moses in the Law and also the prophets wrote, Jesus of Nazareth, the son of Joseph.'

Nathanael said to him, 'Can anything good come out of Nazareth?'

Philip said to him, 'Come and see.'

Jesus saw Nathanael coming towards him and said of him, 'Behold, an Israelite indeed, in whom there is no deceit!'

Nathanael said to him, 'How do you know me?'

Jesus answered him, 'Before Philip called you, when you were under the fig tree, I saw you.'

Nathanael answered him, 'Rabbi, you are the Son of God! You are the King of Israel!'

Jesus answered him, 'Because I said to you, "I saw you under the fig tree," do you believe? You will see greater things than these.'

And he said to him, 'Truly, truly, I say to you, you will see heaven opened, and the angels of God ascending and descending on the Son of Man.'

John 1:43–51

Coming to Christ

The story of any conversion to Christ is an exceedingly personal and intimate matter, involving not merely a person's reason, but that person's spirit and soul, his or her emotions and imagination. For some, conversion is comparatively easy: they come to see themselves as sinners, they discover that Christ and only Christ has the answer to their problem, and in straightforward repentance and simple faith they trust Christ and are saved. With others the process is by no means so simple or direct. They come to Christ through seas of doubts and difficulties, problems and prejudices galore. Nathanael was one such person, and it may well help us if we try and follow him through the maze of thoughts and emotions that he experienced in coming to faith.

Taking the first step

The first step that Nathanael took in the direction of Christ was to give vent to an uninhibited expression of cynicism and doubt. 'Can anything good come out of Nazareth?', said he, biting the head off Philip who had just been trying enthusiastically to evangelize him. It wasn't very courteously put, and it certainly made no attempt to spare the feelings of the would-be evangelist. But it was a step towards Christ. Not a very positive step, you might think, but still a step. Any who take the trouble to think about Christ long enough to begin to see what claims Christ is making, even if they then resent those claims, have begun to move toward Christ. They may turn back at once, but they have taken at least one step.

The trouble with many people is that they have never taken even this first step. They don't believe in Christ, but they don't know why they don't. They have never bothered to think seriously about what he said. They will remark quite knowingly that of course they can't accept that Jesus is the Son of God, because it is intellectually impossible. But they will add that they consider that he was a good man—quite oblivious to the fact that they are revealing by the remark that their intellect has really done remarkably little thinking on the subject at all. If a man claimed to be God, and wasn't, he could by no stretch of imagination be called a good man.

Ever since reports about Christ had been coming his way, Nathanael had at least thought seriously on the matter, but the claims of Christ seemed to him utterly fantastic. And he said so, perhaps quite sharply and with a good deal of sarcasm in his voice. He couldn't help it if his friend felt a bit hurt. Like Nathanael, Philip had been brought up in the centuries old faith of his fathers, with its beautiful and stately rituals, its learned theological discussions in its rabbinical schools led by some of the best trained minds in the country. Philip should have known better than to get mixed up with some backstreet sect.

It wouldn't have been so bad if he had got some new faith that was at least theologically or intellectually respectable. But just listen to him claiming to have found the Messiah, a certain Jesus from *Nazareth* of all places on earth: the idea was laughable. Anyone who knew the slightest thing about the Bible knew that it said that when the Messiah came he would come from Bethlehem, not Nazareth. Of course, you couldn't expect the ordinary people who lived around Nazareth to know much about these things. They were a hot-headed and uneducated crowd: you could tell them any old thing. The more fantastic it was the more they would get carried away with excitement about it. But Philip! Imagine him being taken in by that sort of thing, and getting so enthusiastic about it. 'Philip, man', said Nathanael, 'can any good thing possibly come out of Nazareth?'

Philip's excitement

There's no denying that from one point of view Philip's approach to Nathanael had not been the most tactful. To begin with, although our Lord had been living in Nazareth for some years, so that it was quite natural and correct to speak of him as 'Jesus of Nazareth', he was not born in Nazareth, but in Bethlehem exactly as the prophet Micah had foretold (5:2). Philip might have known that Nathanael was a stickler for getting all the details correct; and there was no point in making it intellectually difficult for him by using loose and inexact phraseology.

And then Philip was so obviously excited, and he should have known that if there was anything that would make Nathanael suspicious, it was excitement and enthusiasm in religion. Nathanael's temperament and taste did not run in that direction. Religion for him was a solemn and stately thing, with ancient musical chants and mournful intoning. And God for him was almighty, distant, remote, awe-inspiring in his greatness and holiness, the very thought of whom made a person serious and subdued. The Messiah, too, as he had been brought up to believe, was a cosmic figure: when he came, he would come in the clouds of heaven. And here was Philip not only claiming that he had come, but talking about him as a someone he knew personally, like his next door neighbour.

Certainly Philip was excited; but then a man who has made the discovery that Philip had just made could scarcely avoid showing some excitement. Some people, if they had merely won three quarters of a million in the lottery, would paint the town red, and no one would think their excitement strange. And yet here was Philip claiming to have discovered the whole secret of history, the purpose of life, the meaning of the world and the significance of the human race! Listen to him as he bursts in on the privacy of Nathanael's shady seat in the garden: 'We have found him of whom Moses in the law and also the prophets wrote, Jesus of Nazareth, the son of Joseph.' Excitement or not, at least Philip was not talking about some little private vision that he himself had thought up. He was claiming to have found the cosmic figure about whom the greatest of Israel's lawgivers and all her prophets had prophesied consistently down the centuries.

Nathanael's idea of truth

Now, being a good Jew, Nathanael believed all this. The disturbing thing about what Philip was saying was that this Saviour of the world had come and, what is more, Philip was absolutely sure he had found him. He sounded all too certain about it. Nathanael, like a good many others, preferred in matters of religion to travel hopefully rather than to arrive. If you were content to tell him you believed that one day God would put the world right, Nathanael was at once prepared to reply that he shared the certain conviction that most likely God would one day perhaps improve things considerably; or at least he felt it was not unreasonable to entertain a distinct hope that he might. But tell Nathanael the Saviour of the world had come, that he could be met personally and you could be sure about it, and Nathanael found it far from attractive. Somehow it took away all the delicious sense of freedom and room for manoeuvre that you had. He didn't mind such talk so long as you could retort, if things began to get too uncomfortable, that of course no one could be sure about these things.

And then, the way Philip put it, the whole thing sounded so directly personal. 'We have found *him*,' he said. Now to pray vaguely for God's kingdom to come, why, there are many decent men and women who would be only too happy to do that. And if it were a question of helping the kingdom of God to come by putting your back into a ten-year plan for agriculture or joining a public-spirited campaign to get an act through parliament banning child pornography, any right-minded person would join it. But to be faced with a person, claiming to be the King himself, and insisting on a one-to-one encounter—that was profoundly disturbing. There would be no knowing what personal claims he might make, what invasions of one's privacy and independence might follow. This was one example of it already. Here he was, trying to get away from things for a while, sitting under the shade of the fig tree in his own private garden, enjoying the peace and privacy of it all, when Philip comes barging in and destroying the calm, not only of the garden but of his mind and conscience, with the troublesome idea that the Saviour of the world was down the street and that Nathanael was invited to meet him personally.

He could, of course, refuse to meet him and stay in the quiet of his garden. But he knew instinctively that that would be the end of any peace for the rest of the day. Conscience would start working overtime, and all kinds of thoughts and emotions chase each other through his head and heart. He knew that this Jesus was a fraud. There was no doubt about it. Still, he had never met him and knew next to nothing about him. How he knew he was a fraud without knowing anything about him was a bit difficult to explain, particularly if he wanted to escape the charge of being prejudiced and obscurantist.

Then there was another thing. It was certainly pleasant sitting under this fig tree. It was, in fact, every Jew's ambition to sit under his own vine and under his own fig tree, as the prophet Micah phrased it (4:4). To enjoy reasonable political freedom, to have enough to live on comfortably with some to spare for the cultural side of life, so that you could sit in your garden in the shade of an old fig tree and savour life a bit—the Jews felt it was everyone's

God-given birthright. And Nathanael had arrived (though multitudes hadn't); he had his own place, and life was tolerably smooth and interesting. But nice as it was, the thought would keep coming: is this all? Is this all that life is about? To have your own house, a wife and pleasant children and then enough to retire on comfortably and to do the things you've always wanted to do, and after that to . . . well, and after that . . . You couldn't live for ever, of course; but was this life all? And what about the millions who didn't manage to make it, so to speak, even in this life, for whom life was little more than a kind of penal servitude in the prison of poverty and ill health? Did the promise of a Saviour of the world amount to no more in the end than the rich sitting under their fig trees and the poor in the labour camps until death put an end to both? If there was only the merest grain of truth in what Philip was saying, it was at least worth investigating seriously.

And so, when in answer to his question, 'Can any good thing come out of Nazareth?', Philip simply said, 'Come and see for yourself', Nathanael got up and went to meet Christ personally.

Face to face with Christ

To be honest, he felt a bit naked leaving the shelter of his fig tree and walking down the middle of the road to meet this person. What was he letting himself in for? Why had he even started out on the road? Why hadn't he stayed behind his doubts? His doubts were good, solid and reasonable doubts, big and respectable enough to hide behind. Whatever was he exposing himself to now? But it was too late to go back, for there standing in front of him was Christ.

Christ was the first to speak. 'That's what I call a real true Israelite,' he said, 'not like old Jacob full of deceit and dishonest pretence. You say exactly what you think, don't you? There's not a drop of guile in you.'

'Rabbi,' said Nathanael politely, 'I wasn't aware that we had met before, how do you know me?'

'Oh, that's all right,' said Christ; 'I saw you before Philip called you. You were sitting under your fig tree, weren't you?'

What happened next is difficult to describe. For Nathanael it was like opening the door to find water outside, which one minute is round your ankles and the next has risen so fast that it is up to your armpits. He had always held it as a religious doctrine, and indeed as a philosophical axiom, that, if there was a God at all, he must be omniscient. But somehow he had never realized it meant *this*. No privacy at all, anywhere? No privacy, not even in your own back garden under your own fig tree? No privacy, not even for your inmost thoughts, or doubts? Nothing but an all-seeing, all-invading God everywhere and at all times?

What happened? Had the heavens suddenly opened and he had been discovered, as an insect is discovered when the stone under which it is hiding is removed? No, as far as he could see, the sky was still the same. It was Christ standing there and focussing all the omniscience of God on Nathanael personally and individually. And strangely enough, he didn't feel in the slightest bit scared. It was a tremendous relief, in fact, to discover that he was known, personally known, and that nothing was hidden and nothing had to be. The doubts, and the sarcasm with which they had been expressed, were all known and accepted as the honest expression of what he had really felt at the time. But more important now was the sense that he, the man behind the doubts, was known and that he was accepted. The God who knew everything about him accepted him in spite of it, and without reproach; so he had no need now to try and hide anything, no need to withdraw behind his doubts to hide. And funny thing: now that he no longer felt any need to hide himself, his doubts were gone. Well, he no longer needed them anyway; he had scarcely noticed them going. Curious! He hadn't always felt like this. What happened? He had come to Christ, and what he had never dreamed of, in a moment, without long argument, he had found.

What had he found? Well, it must be God. Then this was what Philip had meant when he said, 'We have found *him*'. It wasn't presumption or arrogance; it was fact. 'I must have found him, too', Nathanael said to himself. 'Only,' he might have said to Christ, 'if you save me, it's more like being found.'

All this and much more perhaps had gone through Nathanael's mind, though it was only a second or two since Christ had finished speaking. There was no doubt what reply he should make. Steadily, without a quaver of a doubt, he replied, 'Rabbi, you are the Son of God! You are the King of Israel!'

'Yes,' said Christ, 'and let me tell you, you haven't yet discovered a millionth part of what's involved in what you've just said. You shall one day see the heavens opened, and the angels of God ascending and descending on the Son of Man.'

A few brief hours ago and that remark would have made Nathanael feel very uncomfortable. Imagine having every hiding place removed and, whether you were willing to or not, having to look up and see the very face of infinite holiness. Imagine having to do so all unprepared and unreconciled to him, with your conscience witnessing to unforgiven sins, and not having even one doubt thick enough to give even the semblance of cover from the searching eyes. The very idea would have made Nathanael cringe in dread. But that wasn't how he felt about it now. He felt nothing but a surge of wonder and new hope and meaning. He had come to Christ. He was reconciled to God. He had nothing to hide, nothing that he was afraid would one day be discovered. It was all known and forgiven. And now in addition there was something more and even bigger: a future that made sense of life, a future for the world, a future for Nathanael. Let the heavens roll apart here and now; he could scarcely wait! His garden with its fig tree was still quite pleasant, but somehow now it did look a bit small.

STORY TWO

From Water *to* Wine

On the third day there was a wedding at Cana in Galilee, and the mother of Jesus was there. Jesus also was invited to the wedding with his disciples. When the wine ran out, the mother of Jesus said to him, 'They have no wine.'

And Jesus said to her, Woman, what does this have to do with me? My hour has not yet come.'

His mother said to the servants, 'Do whatever he tells you.'

Now there were six stone water jars there for the Jewish rites of purification, each holding twenty or thirty gallons.

Jesus said to the servants, 'Fill the jars with water.' And they filled them up to the brim.

And he said to them, 'Now draw some out and take it to the master of the feast.'

So they took it. When the master of the feast tasted the water now become wine, and did not know where it came from (though the servants who had drawn the water knew), the master of the feast called the bridegroom and said to him, 'Everyone serves the good wine first, and when people have drunk freely, then the poor wine. But you have kept the good wine until now.'

This, the first of his signs, Jesus did at Cana in Galilee, and manifested his glory. And his disciples believed in him.

John 2:1–11

The truth about miracles

The story of the changing of water into wine at the wedding in Cana of Galilee is unashamedly the record of a miracle. In fact, it is one of a series of miracles, or 'signs', recorded by John with the purpose of leading us to 'believe that Jesus is the Christ, the Son of God, and that by believing you may have life in his name' (20:31). In that sense, this story is directed at us, the readers of John's Gospel, and invites us to consider Jesus for ourselves.

At once some will protest that they cannot believe in miracles, and so it is no use reading any further. We must stop a while, therefore, and examine the reasons why they cannot believe in miracles. If we find that we can take seriously what this first sign is saying, then we will be better prepared to listen to what else John will tell us, whether miraculous or otherwise.

Objections to miracles in general

First, some people say that it would be unscientific and therefore intellectually dishonest to believe in miracles; that the physical laws by which the universe runs are quite invariable; and therefore, because miracles go against these physical laws, by definition they cannot happen. In saying this, however, they seem to have forgotten what physical laws are, and who made them. After all, physical laws are not something we find written up on the sky. Physical laws are simply descriptions formulated by humans of what, so far as they can see, normally happens. They deduce these descriptions of what normally happens from studying as much as they can of what goes on.

But what does go on, and what has gone on through these many centuries? You can't decide that by appealing to some law, but only by studying the evidence. Now, there is an enormous amount of evidence to show that miracles have taken place. For instance, the evidence for the resurrection of Christ is overwhelming. If then a scientist or philosopher is willing to put this evidence in front of him along with the evidence for what you might call normal happenings, he will come up with the law that while miracles are not normal happenings, they do sometimes happen. But if he is not prepared to consider the evidence that miracles have happened, but arbitrarily confines himself to studying normal happenings, he will of course come up with a law that miracles don't happen. But his law will not be valid, for his evidence was biased and incomplete. And if he goes further and says that miracles cannot happen, he is not being scientific, but deliberately preventing the facts from speaking.

Objections to this miracle in particular

But granted, someone will say, that it is theoretically possible for miracles to happen occasionally, what evidence have we that this particular miracle of turning water into wine happened? The answer is: very powerful evidence. There is first, the character of John who recorded the miracle. Whatever we may think of the Christian apostles—that they were silly, or deceived—it would be a strange, indeed an impossible, reading of their characters to suggest that they were deliberate liars. John was one of Christ's disciples, and he explicitly says that the disciples were present when the miracle took place. And secondly, behind John and his record stands Jesus Christ himself. He deliberately chose John and the other disciples for this very purpose of witnessing and recording his acts.

But there is another approach along which we can arrive at a decision about the truth of the story. The story offers a diagnosis of one of humanity's basic spiritual diseases. And we can certainly judge whether the diagnosis is correct. It also offers Christ's cure for that disease. It is open to us to try the cure and see if it works. There's nothing like experiencing a miracle to make you sure they can happen.

The miracle of turning water into wine then was not simply an act of supernatural power; it was at the same time an enacted parable. We can see that more easily if we first look at another miracle recorded in this Gospel. Chapter 6 tells us that Christ miraculously multiplied bread and fish, fed the multitude, and then used this physical miracle as an object lesson to bring home to them, and to us, humanity's spiritual hunger and Christ's ability as the bread of life to satisfy that hunger. So it is with the story of the wedding at Cana of Galilee.

When the wine runs out

At this wedding the wine ran out. But then the wine still runs out at many weddings these days. Not the literal wine—that's only there to express the joy of the occasion. The real wine that a wedding celebrates is the joy of the relationship of marriage.

We would be indulging in childish fantasy if we imagined that every marriage led to a conclusion of 'and they lived happily ever after'. The hard facts are that the joy runs out of a good many marriages, and quite a few actually break up. And not only marriages, but other relationships too. Teenagers get fed up with parents, and parents get annoyed and heartbroken over teenagers. Employers get disgusted with employees, and employees lose all patience and confidence in employers. A man will go chasing ambition, only to find that the satisfaction of attainment does not last as long as he thought it would. Young people, pampered by modern affluence, demanding every experience life can give, and getting it all before they are twenty years old, soon discover that their interest has run out. So they become bored and disappointed and feel resentful against life.

The reason the joy goes

Yes, the wine still runs out. But why? We can learn why, if we watch the means Christ used to perform his miracle. You see, he didn't produce wine out of thin air. He didn't even multiply the wine in people's glasses so that it replenished itself as fast as they drank it. No, he got the servants to fill some water jars with water and then he turned this water into wine. Actually, those jars were to hold water for purification, which these people used as a religious duty. Being decent folk they had doubtless also had some kind of religious ceremony at the wedding; but for the moment that was all over, and now they were getting on with the fun. Christ used these religious water jars as vehicles for the renewed joy of the party. Quietly, but effectively, he was giving them, and us, a very telling object lesson that would preach its own sermon as they reflected on it in later days.

Let me illustrate the point. Suppose a woman has a daughter whose face keeps breaking out with sores. She brings the doctor in to have a look at the child and find out what's wrong. Presently without saying a word the doctor goes and gets the bread bin, takes the lid off and sets it in the middle of the lounge floor. Mother looks in and sees to her horror that the bread bin is alive with dirt and maggots! It hasn't been cleaned out for ages. The doctor doesn't need to say anything. By dragging that bread bin into the centre of the situation, he gives a silent but eloquent diagnosis of the trouble and puts his finger on the cause of the girl's illness.

The cure Christ offers

So it was with Christ and these water jars. They were there for the purpose of purification; not simply for hygiene either, but for religious purification. With the wedding feast in full swing, they would have been left very much on the fringe of the party. And they were empty, too. Christ begins by bringing them to the fore and ordering them to be filled. He is offering us, in the language of parable, his diagnosis of our trouble. We are not clean. Our personal hygiene may be all that could be desired, but spiritually in God's sight we are far from clean.

We like to think of course that we are decent—we wouldn't blaspheme, or anything like that. In fact, we go to church sometimes, particularly at weddings and funerals, and even on a few Sundays when we don't actually have to. But, if we're truthful, for the rest of life we leave God very much out in the cold. Perhaps on holidays we make a distant and very polite bow in his direction; but we wouldn't think of making him the centre of our hearts and activities. Why, if a guest got up at a wedding reception and began to say that the secret of lasting joy is to receive Christ personally as Saviour, and began to illustrate the point by recounting the story of his own personal experience of conversion to Christ, how many of the parents and guests would hear him through without getting most uncomfortably embarrassed? He might well be told afterwards that church is the place, if anywhere, to talk about things like that, and that he had no right to ruin people's fun by dragging God and religion into a wedding reception.

And then we wonder why life goes sour on us, and its joy doesn't last! How could it do otherwise, when we treat the Almighty in this fashion? He made us; he has given us every beautiful and joyful thing we have, and yet we persist in keeping him at arm's length and cutting ourselves off from any real friendship and fellowship with him. And it is pathetically inadequate to think that, as long as we are decent and behave courteously, God will be satisfied. What would you think of a young man who from the time he was married treated his wife with great courtesy—always getting up and offering her his seat when she entered the room, and always opening the door for her when she went out—but never loved her passionately with all his heart, mind, soul and strength? Would not his mere courtesy make a travesty of the relationship? And God our maker, who has given us proof of his love in a thousand ways, will not be fobbed off with mere courtesy and decency. He expects us to love him with all our heart, mind, soul and strength, and he regards our failure to love him like this as our most grievous sin, and the root of all the others.

What it will take

But somebody will say: 'You can't make yourself love God. If you don't love him, you just don't love him, and that's all there is to it.' Sadly enough, that's very true. Sin and selfishness have not only defiled our hearts, they have bankrupted them; and the fact that we do not love our creator more than anyone or anything else is an indication of how far things have gone wrong. Can they be put right? Yes. Most emphatically yes! But it will take a miracle to do it, and Christ doesn't try to hide that fact from us. Quite the reverse. In fact, he tells us bluntly that the best we can do in the way of moral reform by our own natural effort is inadequate. We need the miracle of regeneration, performed within us by the Holy Spirit: forgiving, cleansing, enlightening, empowering. And above all, putting us right with God, so that the springs of our thoughts, actions and relationships may be purified and a new kind and quality of life given to us. A miracle in fact; not a physical one of turning water into wine, but that spiritual miracle of which Christ spoke when he said,

> Truly, truly, I say to you, unless one is born of water and the Spirit, he cannot enter the kingdom of God. That which is born of the flesh is flesh, and that which is born of the Spirit is spirit. Do not marvel that I said to you, 'You must be born again.' (John 3:5–7)

Born of water and of the Spirit, what does it mean? We will think about those verses in their context in the next chapter, but here we have an illustration to help us begin to think about them.

The water jars that Christ used to perform his miracle of turning water into wine held about twenty gallons each, and there were six of them. One hundred and twenty gallons then, all told; it was rather a lot of water to have around the place, especially when you remember that it was for use in some kind of religious purification. And it was rather chilly stuff, too: there was no joy in it. What was worse was that, for all its large amount, it was inadequate.

More than washing with water

What help or joy can religious ceremonies and ceremonial water give us? After all, the real human plight that we are discussing goes very deep. Our problem is that the wine of life's joy runs out because human relationships become sour and embittered, and this is because of our deep-lying selfishness, peevishness, jealousy, envy, cruelty, ingratitude, cowardice, pride, and above all because our sinfulness has ruined our relation with God. What can water do about that? Very little or nothing.

It is true that the Old Testament speaks of ceremonial washings in water, and the New Testament requires people, once they have received Christ, to be baptized in water. But neither one nor the other claims that this water does anything to deal with the cause of our spiritual trouble. The Old Testament washings in water cleansed the skin from ceremonial defilement contracted by touching a dead body or something like that. But our spiritual uncleanness lies far deeper than the skin, and no water can reach it. For it is not what touches a person's skin or goes into a person's stomach that defiles them; it is what comes out of their corrupt and sinful hearts (Mark 7:18-23).

Christian baptism too is only a symbol, by which a Christian confesses and illustrates the change that came about when he or she received the Saviour. But until a person receives the Saviour, there is no change there to symbolize, and a thousand baptisms would never bring the change about.

It will take a miracle

We need to be very clear about this. Christ offers us a miracle of regeneration, giving us new life, but he performs no magic. Yet it is surprising how many people there are even in this modern age who still regard baptism as a kind of magic. You will hear now and again of an argument between some parents and a clergyman who has refused to baptize their infant because the parents never go to church. It is quite clear that such parents regard baptism as some kind of magic that somehow communicates some benefit to the child without the child's personal faith, or the parents' either. And there are many other people who base their hope for eventual acceptance with God on the fact that in the dim and distant past they underwent some similar ceremony. It is nothing but superstition; and if we are going to be realists and face the realities of our condition, we shall have to give up these mediaeval superstitions and recognize that spiritual trouble can only be cured by spiritual means. Unless we do, the result can only be either self-deception or else cynical disillusionment.

The cleansing that Christ brings is a spiritual cleansing and it is brought about by spiritual means. Hear it described in the words of the Apostle Paul.

> But when the goodness and loving kindness of God our Saviour appeared, he saved us, not because of works done by us in righteousness, but according to his own mercy, by the washing of regeneration and renewing of the Holy Spirit, whom he poured out on us richly through Jesus Christ our Saviour, so that being justified by his grace we might become heirs according to the hope of eternal life. (Titus 3:4–7)

Paul's experience was certainly outstanding, but it was not meant to be unique. In fact, the Bible says that his experience is basically the pattern along which God saves and changes everyone who trusts the Saviour.

You may think that all this talk about conversion to Christ, salvation and forgiveness is rather chilly, watery stuff. But people who have actually experienced it know that Christ turns the process of saving and cleansing them into the very wine of lasting joy.

So it was with David, the ancient Jewish king. Under temptation he committed adultery, and trying to cover it up he got involved in indirect murder. For a time, he tried to tell himself that it didn't matter; at some time everybody gets mixed up like this, and so forth. But conscience and the worry of it began to affect him in both his body and his mind. He couldn't sleep and he couldn't eat, and he developed all kinds of mysterious ailments. Then, to cut a long story short, God brought him to repentance and to confession of his sin, and faith brought him the assurance of forgiveness and acceptance with God.[1] Well, when that happened, he went home with such deep joy welling up in his heart, that he sat down and immediately wrote a poem about his experience. He set it to music, got out his harp and sang and played for all he was worth. The words were: 'Oh, the sheer happiness of the man whose sin is forgiven, whose transgression is covered; Oh, the sheer happiness of the man to whom the Lord imputes not iniquity!' (see Psa 32:1–2; Rom 4:6–8).

John Newton, of more recent times, was a brutal, foul-mouthed, captain of a slave ship. He too found forgiveness and the cleansing of the new birth. In his gratitude he wrote a hymn in the words of which he and millions after him have expressed their response of love to the Saviour:

> How sweet the name of Jesus sounds
> In a believer's ear!
> It soothes his sorrows, heals his wounds,
> And drives away his fear.

The fear that personal commitment to Christ is a chilly experience that will drag a wet blanket over life's joys is an empty fear. As they will tell you themselves, people who accept Christ's diagnosis and experience his cure discover that he turns the process of his spiritual cleansing of their lives into the source of their greatest joy.

---

1   You can read the whole story in 2 Sam 11–12.

From Studying God *to* Knowing Him

CHRIST'S CONVERSATION
WITH NICODEMUS

The Passover of the Jews was at hand, and Jesus went up to Jerusalem. In the temple he found those who were selling oxen and sheep and pigeons, and the money-changers sitting there. And making a whip of cords, he drove them all out of the temple, with the sheep and oxen. And he poured out the coins of the money-changers and overturned their tables. And he told those who sold the pigeons, 'Take these things away; do not make my Father's house a house of trade.' His disciples remembered that it was written, 'Zeal for your house will consume me.'

So the Jews said to him, 'What sign do you show us for doing these things?'

Jesus answered them, 'Destroy this temple, and in three days I will raise it up.'

The Jews then said, 'It has taken forty-six years to build this temple, and will you raise it up in three days?' But he was speaking about the temple of his body. When therefore he was raised from the dead, his disciples remembered that he had said this, and they believed the Scripture and the word that Jesus had spoken.

Now when he was in Jerusalem at the Passover Feast, many believed in his name when they saw the signs that he was doing. But Jesus on his part did not entrust himself to them, because he knew all people and needed no one to bear witness about man, for he himself knew what was in man.

Now there was a man of the Pharisees named Nicodemus, a ruler of the Jews. This man came to Jesus by night and said to him, 'Rabbi, we know that you are a teacher come from God, for no one can do these signs that you do unless God is with him.'

Jesus answered him, 'Truly, truly, I say to you, unless one is born again he cannot see the kingdom of God.'

Nicodemus said to him, 'How can a man be born when he is old? Can he enter a second time into his mother's womb and be born?'

Jesus answered, 'Truly, truly, I say to you, unless one is born of water and the Spirit, he cannot enter the kingdom of God. That which is born of the flesh is flesh, and that which is born of the Spirit is spirit. Do not marvel that I said to you, 'You must be born again.' The wind blows where it wishes, and you hear its sound, but you do not know where it comes from or where it goes. So it is with everyone who is born of the Spirit.'

Nicodemus said to him, 'How can these things be?'

Jesus answered him, 'Are you the teacher of Israel and yet you do not understand these things? Truly, truly, I say to you, we speak of what we know, and bear witness to what we have seen, but you do not receive our testimony. If I have told you earthly things and you do not believe, how can you believe if I tell you heavenly things? No one has ascended into heaven except he who descended from heaven, the Son of Man. And as Moses lifted up the serpent in the wilderness, so must the Son of Man be lifted up, that whoever believes in him may have eternal life. For God so loved the world, that he gave his only Son, that whoever believes in him should not perish but have eternal life.'

'For God did not send his Son into the world to condemn the world, but in order that the world might be saved through him. Whoever believes in him is not condemned, but whoever does not believe is condemned already, because he has not believed in the name of the only Son of God. And this is the judgement: the light has come into the world, and people loved the darkness rather than the light because their works were evil. For everyone who does wicked things hates the light and does not come to the light, lest his works should be exposed. But whoever does what is true comes to the light, so that it may be clearly seen that his works have been carried out in God.'

John 2:13–3:21

Commercializing the way to God

According to Ephesians 2, salvation is a free gift (vv. 4–10), but there is something about the human spirit, whether pride or fear, who knows, that will not have it so, but will insist on trying to earn it or pay for it in one form or another. Some will think it necessary to pay in the currency of good behaviour or merit; others imagine that if they can work up within themselves perfect love of God this will induce God to forgive them; still others will offer God literal currency to buy release from the guilt of their sins. And it is all a tragic mistake, for salvation cannot be purchased.

The idea that it can be bought is in itself a fundamental sin: it assumes that we created beings have some resources that are our own (which would not be true even if we were sinless) and it disguises the true fact that we are morally bankrupt. So it keeps us back from that radical repentance that owns our own complete unworthiness, acknowledges God's judgment as just, and humbly takes as an unmerited gift the salvation that God through Christ offers for free.

Analyzing the reasons why the majority of the Jews of his day were not saved, Paul attributes it to this false attitude of imagining that they could earn salvation by their merit. 'Seeking to establish their own [righteousness],' he says, 'they did not submit to God's righteousness' (Rom 10:3). It was a great pity then that the very priests in the temple had connived at the commercialization of the services and so helped to strengthen in the people this erroneous idea that they could buy, earn or merit salvation.

Loving the symbol but missing the reality

One other sad feature showed itself on this occasion in the temple when Christ cleansed it. When in answer to their request for a sign he said, 'Destroy this temple, and I will raise it up in three days', the Jews did not understand what he meant. They could not be blamed for that. The sad thing however is that they were not even interested to ask what he meant. At this time they were celebrating the Passover, remembering the experience of God's power that had brought their forefathers out of Egypt. Now in their midst stood one whose action had given strong evidence even to them that he was the one of whom Malachi had prophesied when he said, 'the Lord whom you seek shall suddenly come to his temple . . . and he will purify the sons of Levi and refine them like gold and silver' (see 3:1, 3). He talked to them, albeit in cryptic language, of more than human power, and of a temple raised in virtue of that power. What experience was this? What new and vigorous worship did it foretell? They were not interested to find out. All they could think of was their temple of stone. In their eyes it was a marvel. It had been in the process of building for forty-six years (the tourists were generally opened mouthed when they were told this); it cost who knows how many millions and still was not finished (at this the flow of tourists' money into the collection boxes increased noticeably). What could Jesus, or the Messiah himself, offer anyone that was better than this impressive pile of stones, with its magnificent art, its colourful ritual, and the religious bric-a-brac on sale at the door? They were not interested to find out.

And it is not only Jews who need to be saved from this attitude. Writing to Gentiles in Ephesus who had recently been converted from the worship of Diana and the temple that was one of the wonders of the world, Paul confessed that he prayed for them regularly that

> the God of our Lord Jesus Christ, the Father of glory, may give you the spirit of wisdom and of revelation in the knowledge of him, having the eyes of your hearts enlightened, that you may know . . . what is the immeasurable greatness of his power towards us who believe . . . that he worked in Christ when he raised him from the dead and seated him at his right hand in the heavenly places . . . and seated us with him . . . (see Eph 1:15–2:7)

This too is, or seems to be, cryptic language: for in what sense has the power of God raised not only Christ from the dead and set him at his own right hand, but the believer as well? But if we want our Christian worship to be more than a formality, we must not be content until our eyes are in fact opened to know what it means.

And so during the feast Christ did many signs of miraculous power in the city to encourage people to enquire and seek God personally and to find the spiritual power that alone can make the worship of God a living reality. There were some of course who were impressed by the miracles simply as exciting and sensational religious shows. We are told that Christ did not commit himself to them (John 2:23–25). He was not interested then, any more than he is now, in simply providing people with religious entertainment and emotional excitement. The external acts of power were simply meant as pointers to God's offer of power at a far deeper, more significant, spiritual level; power that would transform a person's character, that would give a person the ability to understand the things of God. There were some who realized that the miracles must have some such deeper purpose, and they came to Christ personally to find out what it was. In fact, as we read John's third chapter we find one such man coming to Jesus by night to talk over the significance of the signs. We must do our best to listen in on the conversation.

A man who came with his questions

To a sensitive academic theologian like Nicodemus the commercialization of religion in the temple must have been extremely repulsive, and Christ's action in casting it out would have commended itself to his conscience as soon as he heard of it. When there followed a steady stream of reports that this young man Jesus was performing miraculous deeds that were not simply exhibitions of power but seemed to carry weighty spiritual lessons, the urge within Nicodemus to investigate the phenomenon became overpowering. Even so, the decision to seek a personal interview with Christ was not an easy one for him to make. It would raise more than eyebrows if it came to the notice of his colleagues that he had begun to take seriously the claims of Jesus to be the Messiah and had actually gone to have a personal conversation with him. It would raise a question mark over the soundness of his scholarly judgment. Of course, if he had been doing some research on 'The Growth and Development of the Messianic Idea in the Period of the Early Monarchy', that would have been regarded as an admirably sound topic for a scholar to devote himself to. But to suppose it was possible that the Messiah had actually come and that he was a carpenter from Galilee without an hour's training in theology would be automatically regarded as evidence of the worst possible taste in religion, and a sad lapse of true critical judgment.

'But,' he could hear himself arguing back at his colleagues, 'what about these signs that Jesus is doing day after day? Is it sound academic practice to refuse to examine evidence and to base one's conclusions on prejudice of *a priori* considerations? Suppose he does come from Galilee and suppose he is only a carpenter; wasn't one of our great prophets, Amos, only a shepherd? And don't our students nowadays get PhDs for investigating the theology and the social conscience of Amos and so forth?'

But it was no use; his arguments would have made no difference. Amos was a figure from the ancient past: it was therefore respectable to investigate him, even if he was only a shepherd. But a carpenter in the present claiming to be the Messiah, to be the Saviour of the nation and of the world, a someone you had to trust in to be saved—there were some things that any sound academic would instinctively know were unworthy of investigation. And at any rate, the assured results of modern biblical study, which all scholars accepted, were that there were no grounds for thinking that any prophet would come out of Galilee (see 7:52). To question this majority view must mean that a man was no scholar; or at least, if he were, that he was very eccentric.

No, it was not going to be easy for Nicodemus to take the step of seeking out Christ personally, and general public meetings were so unsatisfactory, in that they raised so many questions that were never answered. What for instance would this young man say about the idea that appealed to a number of scholars that, according to the Old Testament, one might expect two Messiahs—one of the house of Judah and one of the house of Joseph? And what did he make of the interesting new suggestion that the whole Messianic promise needed to be demythologized before one could rightly understand it? For it was a crude literalism to suppose that when the Bible prophesied that Messiah would come riding into Jerusalem on a donkey, it meant that Messiah would come riding into Jerusalem on a donkey! One should rather understand that it meant if all Israel were humble and kept the law for one day, that would constitute the coming of Messiah: not the coming of a person, but the spread of an attitude of humility and truthfulness. Did it not?

He really must seek out this young man and put some of these questions to him. Undeniably the young man was doing some remarkable miracles; but then was his theology intellectually sound? And how could you find that out if you did not go and speak with him? Of one thing he was certain: to devote the strength of one's manhood to the academic study of the Bible and biblical theology, and then when there was evidence to suggest that God was in fact alive and actively working in the world, to refuse even to investigate the evidence was to make a nonsense out of one's whole professional life. And so, with the indirect courage that some nervous people possess, he set out one night after dark to seek a personal interview with Christ.

The conversation

Nicodemus apparently began the conversation. 'Rabbi,' he said; and there was not the slightest trace of condescension in his voice, and certainly none of sarcasm, as he used the title to address the younger, non-academic man. Nicodemus was a scholar, not a narrow-minded professional. 'Rabbi, we know that you are a teacher come from God, for no one can do these signs that you do unless God is with him' (3:2).

But to tell a man that you know he is a teacher is normally the preamble to asking him a question and inviting him to give the answer. What question was Nicodemus planning to ask? Was it perhaps, 'What, if I may ask, are your views on the Messianic question? You wouldn't suppose, would you, that all the messianic Scriptures are to be interpreted literally? Or would you?' Actually, we shall never know what he was planning to ask. There are some approaches to the knowledge of God and salvation that are bound to be sterile; and before he could embark on any such approach, our Lord cut him short. Nicodemus had come stating what he knew: 'we know that you are a teacher come from God.' Then he must let the teacher dictate what the first lesson should be. And it turned out to be the most elementary lesson possible: 'Jesus answered him, "Truly, truly, I say to you, unless one is born again he cannot see the kingdom of God"' (3:3).

The directness of this approach must have stunned Nicodemus; and it may well stun us, if we pause long enough to realize the implications of it. If one is going to discuss the kingdom of God at all, one can scarcely get a more elementary lesson than that which explains the basic condition to be fulfilled before a person can either enter or even see that kingdom. Why was Christ choosing to begin the conversation with this senior theologian by solemnly enunciating this basic and elementary lesson? The answer is simple, but profoundly disquieting: this theologian, for all his learning, was an unregenerate man. He had never been born again.

Accepting substitutes for reality

The revelation once made, however shocking, helps to explain an earlier problem. All that commercialization of religion that had been going on in the temple—where did it all come from? Nicodemus might have disapproved of it, but was he not in part responsible for it? If he had never himself been born again, it is certain that he had never taught the priests that they needed to be born again, nor the people either. And if people have never been born again, even if they try to worship and serve God, they will not, as Christ puts it, be able to 'see the kingdom of God'. The things of God will be incomprehensible to them (see 1 Cor 2:14); and they will therefore substitute a number of lesser things for spiritual fellowship with God. Some will imagine that the aesthetic experience of listening to a trained choir is a spiritual experience, and they will transform divine service into a sacred concert. Others will imagine that the intellectual stimulus of theoretical theology is a spiritual thing, and they will perhaps become academic theologians. But the masses who have little interest in aesthetics and less still in intellect, will demand something coarser and less sophisticated. Superstition and commerce together will supply it.

Born again

As Nicodemus was recovering from his surprise at Christ's statement, he asked: 'How can a man be born when he is old? Can he enter a second time into his mother's womb and be born?' (John 3:4). It is possible to suppose that Nicodemus really thought Christ meant a literal physical birth, and that he was questioning its possibility. Yet while Nicodemus was an unregenerate man, there is no need to insult his intelligence by making that supposition. Maybe he thought Christ was preaching a solution to humanity's problems that was impractical, some wild fairy-story of a theology like minor sects are liable to think up every now and again; and perhaps he was politely pooh-poohing its impracticability. Perhaps it is most likely that our Lord's words about being born again had prompted in him the wistful longing that we all may have felt, although we know it is impossible: 'Oh, if I could only start all over again.' It is not only that we have done a lot of things that now we wish we had not. It is also that we ourselves are now made up of a tangle of memories, habits and complexes that give our behaviour a constant and perverse twist however hard we try to correct it. How wonderful it would be, we think, if we could go back to the start and be born over again. It is impossible, of course, and much as Nicodemus may have wished that it were possible, he knew it wasn't.

It was not only impossible: in the sense that Nicodemus was thinking of, it would have been useless, even if it were possible. To be born all over again as a baby with the same kind of life as we had the first time, and the same nature, why, that would simply lead to the same result all over again. Immediately therefore our Lord replied with an amplification of his original statement, which made it clear that by being born again, he did not mean returning to the beginnings of a new unspoiled human life, but being born into a new category of life. 'Unless one is born of water and the Spirit,' he said, 'he cannot enter the kingdom of God.' Then he added the reason why that is so: 'That which is born of the flesh is flesh, and that which is born of the Spirit is spirit. Do not marvel that I said to you, "You must be born again"' (3:5–7).

The first time we were born we were born flesh. Since then, the flesh has, so to speak, got sorely damaged and defiled. Christ's demand is not for the flesh to be taken back to the innocence of its babyhood. He is demanding another birth of a different kind: a birth that will commence within us a spiritual life, just as our physical birth produced our fleshly life. Of course you cannot see with your eyes a spiritual birth take place. But that does not mean it is not real. It is as real a thing as a physical birth. 'The wind', said Christ to Nicodemus, 'blows where it will; you hear the sound of it, but you cannot tell where it started and where it will end up' (see v. 8). Yet no one would think of suggesting that the wind is only something that we imagine, or merely a concept. It is as real as things we can see. And so it is with the new life that begins to live within the person who is born again. From that point on there exists within them a life that was not there before.

A wrong idea about washing and the new birth

Nicodemus found all this very hard to grasp. 'How can these things be?' he said. And not only him. Mediaeval Christendom made basically the same mistake as Nicodemus, and what is more, built it into its theology and rituals.

First it supposed that when our Lord talked of being born of water he was referring to the rite of infant baptism. And then it supposed, in addition, that being born again meant being cleansed from the taint of Adam our forefather's sin: a baby being born had a nature, a flesh, to use the technical term, tainted by the inherited stain of Adam's sin, but baptism would wash away that taint and stain and so restore the baby to original purity. Thereafter all that was needed was for the grace of God gradually to perfect nature, which is the very opposite of what our Lord taught. Suppose you could cleanse the flesh from the taint of Adam's sin, (and, of course, you cannot), it would still be flesh even then. It might be clean flesh, pure flesh, innocent flesh, but it would still be flesh. And what Christ was, and still is, demanding was not an improvement of the flesh, but the birth of an altogether different and higher kind of life: 'That which is born of the flesh is flesh, and that which is born of the Spirit is spirit.'

Water and the Spirit

As we observed in our last chapter, it would be little more than a superstition to suppose that the birth of a spiritual life could be effected within a baby or an adult by means of literal water, however much prayed over and sanctified for the purpose that water was. Nicodemus himself, since he was a Jew, and used to endless washings in literal water in the course of his religious rites, would have (or at least could have) known better than that if he simply recalled his own Jewish Scriptures. Indeed, our Lord gently expressed his surprise that a learned biblical scholar like Nicodemus should not already be conversant with the need for and the meaning of the new birth. 'Are you the teacher of Israel and yet you do not understand these things?' How many times must Nicodemus have read and studied the famous chapters in the prophecy of Ezekiel that predict the rebirth of Israel! In one of the chapters the prophet records his vision of a valley of dry bones, about which and to which he was commanded to announce the word of the Lord. Presently he saw with astonishment the bones assemble themselves into bodies and flesh, and sinews clothe the bony skeletons. And then he was commanded to prophesy.

> Then he said to me, 'Prophesy to the breath [or, wind]; prophesy, son of man, and say to the breath [or, wind], Thus says the Lord GOD: 'Come from the four winds, O breath [or, spirit], and breathe on these slain, that they may live.' So I prophesied as he commanded me, and the breath came into them, and they lived . . . (Ez 37:9–10)[1]

Nicodemus must have read it many times; and now here was Christ using the literal wind and its mysterious comings and goings, as an illustration of the power of the Holy Spirit's action in regeneration, imparting new life where there had been no life before, just as God had done through the prophet. Why did he not understand? Again, in the previous chapter Ezekiel had voiced God's promise to Israel.

> I will sprinkle clean water on you, and you shall be clean from all your uncleannesses, and from all your idols I will cleanse you. And I will give you a new heart, and a new spirit I will put within you. (36:25–26)

'Water and the Spirit'—Nicodemus should have recognized the words at once, and as a teacher of theology he ought long since to have pondered their significance. Here was water mentioned that could cleanse Israel from her filthiness and idolatry. What water? The literal water of some ceremonial bath or baptism? Hardly. Ceremonial washings, ablutions and baptisms in literal water had been instituted by God as part of the symbols of Israel's religious system from the time of Moses. By Ezekiel's time there would not have been a person in the whole nation who had not been many times washed and sprinkled. Yet they were abominably filthy: through chapter after chapter of Ezekiel's prophecy God is heard denouncing their uncleanness, and warning of the terrible consequences that were about to follow. The ceremonial washings had been remarkably ineffective. When

---

1   The Hebrew word for spirit, *ruach*, can also be translated as either 'breath' or 'wind'.

therefore God announced his promise of the eventual spiritual rebirth of the nation, was he really promising that the literal water of their ceremonial washings and sprinklings, which had failed a million times to remove spiritual defilement, was somehow going to be successful on the million and first occasion? Obviously not. As with all the symbols of Israel's religion, so with this one: the symbol itself effected nothing. Its sole purpose was to point to the spiritual reality.

Word and the Spirit

Christians likewise may know from their apostles and prophets just what our Lord meant by water when he talked of being born of water and the Spirit. Hear the Apostle Peter on regeneration: 'you have been born again, not of perishable seed but of imperishable, through the living and abiding word of God' (1 Pet 1:23). Hear the Apostle John: 'No one born of God makes a practice of sinning, for God's seed abides in him' (1 John 3:9).

So Peter and John are both agreed. The new life imparted in regeneration springs from the seed of God, which is conveyed through the word of God. Listen to our Lord further describe that word: 'The words that I have spoken to you are spirit and life' (John 6:63). That is to say, our Lord's words did not merely convey information; they were living and creative, they conveyed life, they were life. Now hear Paul as he talks of the cleansing element in that same word: 'having cleansed her [the church] by the washing of water with the word' (Eph 5:26). And listen to him again on this same matter of regeneration: 'he saved us . . . by the washing of regeneration and renewal of [that is, performed by] the Holy Spirit' (Titus 3:5). Notice particularly what it is that is said to be poured upon us to effect the washing of regeneration. It is not the literal water of baptism, but the Holy Spirit.

But how, someone will say, can water be a term for both the word, as in Ephesians 5, and the Spirit, as in Titus 3? The answer is to be found in the saying of our Lord's which we have just quoted from John 6:63. The words of Christ are spirit: they are the words of the living God, conceived in the Spirit of God and spoken in the power of the Spirit of God. The words are not thus separable from the Holy Spirit who speaks them.

The Holy Spirit performs many ministries. When he imparts life, terms like *seed* and *word* are used; when he effects cleansing, the terms *water* and *washing* are used; when he burns up evil in judgment, the term *fire* is used. So John the Baptist prophesied that our Lord would baptize people in the Holy Spirit and in fire (Matt 3:11), while our Lord tells Nicodemus and us all that we must be born of water and the Spirit. Happily enough, Christendom has never got round to turning the baptism 'in the Spirit and in fire' into a ceremony in which literal fire is used. It would have saved endless confusion, frustration and disillusionment if Christendom had never tried to turn regeneration into a ceremony in which literal water is used. Nothing could be more important or vital than entry into the kingdom of God. The alternative to entry is unthinkable. On this matter we cannot afford to confuse ourselves or others with empty and misleading symbols. Nothing but the actual reality will do. Let Christ himself tell us, 'Truly, truly, I say to you, unless one is born again he cannot see the kingdom of God.'

A clear difficulty

For Nicodemus it was all very disconcerting. In the first place he just did not understand what the young prophet was saying. It wasn't that the words he used were difficult or that his language was intricate and philosophical. Indeed, if it had been Nicodemus would have found it easier: he would have understood it and enjoyed it. More than likely there was nothing he enjoyed more than discussing a really difficult crux of interpretation, where one had to be careful to define one's terms with the utmost nicety and balance the arguments with judicious care. Of course, in the seminars of the theological school you had to be very bright sometimes even to appreciate the point and subtlety of some of the arguments; and you could easily make yourself look a fool in the eyes of the students if you failed to see the point of your opponent's position. Not that it worried Nicodemus a lot: he wasn't *the* teacher of Israel for nothing.

But in what this young prophet was saying there was nothing you could argue about. 'You must be born again,' he asserted, 'or else you cannot see the kingdom of God.' It was a shockingly extreme statement and so directly personal. It made you ask yourself, 'Well, have I been born again? Either I have or I haven't.' It was no good replying, 'In a way I think I may have been.' And it was getting pretty evident what the young man thought about him.

A question of understanding

So the best thing would be to keep the discussion more on the impersonal and objective level. But then that was precisely what it was so difficult to do. If someone asserts that it is wrong to paint pictures on the Sabbath, because painting pictures is work, there you have the makings of a really good discussion. You can first debate what constitutes work. You can then argue whether painting is work or recreation, and so on and so forth. But suppose someone says, 'There is a drawing on this piece of paper, but you cannot see it and never will unless you look at it under ultraviolet light. I can take you to a source of ultraviolet light and show you the picture, if you will follow me.' What is there that you can debate about that? You could of course refuse to believe that there is a drawing on the paper, and you could baldly deny that there is such a thing as ultraviolet light. And you could conclude that the man who claims there is a picture there is a trickster or a lunatic. But even that is a difficult thing to do, particularly if you are not quite sure what ultraviolet light is, and if in addition the man in front of you seems in other respects to be a remarkably competent scientist. Really the thing to do is simply to say, 'All right; take me to this source of ultraviolet light and show me the picture.' If it turns out that he is a liar, there is nothing lost. However, it would mean trusting the man at least initially to the point of following him down the street to the laboratory. And what a fool you would look if he turned out to be a fraud. Perhaps there is one thing you could do. You could say, 'I don't understand how this ultraviolet light you talk of could possibly reveal a picture that is not visible to ordinary eyesight. I can't see how it works.' Wouldn't that be a good enough excuse for not going down to the laboratory to see whether it works or not?

'I just don't understand how these things you speak of could possibly come about', said Nicodemus.

'True,' said Christ, 'you do not understand. But your basic problem is not that you don't *understand*. The trouble with you is that you won't *believe*. Even things that you can check and know to be true you are not prepared to believe. Truly, truly, I say to you, what we are telling you is something we know about. We are witnessing to something that we have actually seen. And you do not receive our testimony. We are not offering you a thesis to be debated, but making an eyewitness statement for you to test. But you will not even admit our testimony; you will not receive it. Some of the things I have told you have been earthly things, like the movements of the wind, that you can know from your own experience. But even those you are not prepared to trust far enough to begin to think that there might be an analogy between the action of the invisible wind in the physical sphere and the movements of the Spirit in the invisible spiritual realm. And if I have told you earthly things and you won't believe, how shall you believe if I tell you heavenly things? Nicodemus you are really an unbeliever' (see John 3:11–12).

The learned rabbi flinched, but he made no protest. The arrow had got in before he had time to erect his defences, and with the sudden dawning of self-knowledge the wound was beginning to smart. An unbeliever? He, Nicodemus, a theologian of many years standing! Where would these allegations stop? First to have it hinted that he was an unregenerate man, and now to be told outright that he was not a believer: he ought surely to protest at the liberties this young man was taking.

A question of trust

Self-knowledge took away any heart he might have had in making a protest. Yes, of course, in a very real sense he was a believer: he believed that there was a God. He believed that the Bible was the word of God—why else had he devoted his whole life to the study of it? But it was true, if he was like many who wrestle with such issues, that there was another sense in which he found it difficult to believe anything far enough to commit himself on it. In the council meetings of the Sanhedrin, for example, even when he felt he had a strong case, he found it impossibly difficult to commit himself to it unreservedly. He would hesitate and hesitate—while some of his colleagues would say the first thing that came into their heads with all the self-confidence in the world. And at length when he did manage to blurt out something he would scarcely get to the end of the second sentence before he could see another possible point of view, and his statement would go trailing off into inarticulate silence. (You can see an actual instance of this in 7:45–52). That is why he enjoyed discussions and debates so much, so long as he did not have to commit himself to any one view and act upon it. Why could you not qualify for entry into God's kingdom by knowing your theology well? He himself knew every system of theology there was, and could argue the strong and weak points of them all.

Why must you commit yourself by believing firmly in some one of them, as this young man seemed to say? And anyway who was this young man to talk to him like this? He seemed so confident, so dogmatic. There he goes again: 'Truly, truly, I say to you.' That was the third time he had used the phrase in the conversation so far. It was one thing to admit, as Nicodemus had done, that he was a teacher come from God. But then all the other teachers he had ever known in the theological schools (and he had known some very famous teachers) always spoke so very humbly, and rarely said anything for which they could not cite the authority of some earlier rabbi. Here was this young man, and he had not quoted a rabbinical authority yet. Instead, this constant and confident, 'Truly, truly, *I say* to you.' Had he, Nicodemus, a learned rabbi and senior professor in the college, got to believe this young man, whatever he said simply because he said it?

'Yes, that's exactly how you will have to believe,' said Christ, 'if ever you are to know about heavenly things. For no man has ascended into heaven, except he that descended out of heaven, even the Son of Man. He alone therefore can tell you about heavenly things, and the only way you will ever get to know about them is by trusting him' (see John 3:12–13).

And this must be so. Theology, when all is said and done, professes to be the study of God. But God is not a philosophical or theological proposition to be debated; he is a person to be trusted. Indeed, there is no way of getting to know a person in the fullest sense of the term without trusting that person. And the heart of the human predicament is not that we do not *know* enough, but that we do not *trust* God. Eve started it all—being deceived into ceasing to trust God's word and God himself (Gen 3). And we have all gone astray down the same byroad, and got ourselves lost. If ever we are to be saved, it will not be primarily by solving some theological problem to our intellectual satisfaction; it will be by being brought to believe God and trust him. Nor is it a question of one theologian dogmatically asserting his theological view over against other views. It is a question of God himself 'coming down' from heaven as Son of Man to speak with men and women and so lead them to faith in himself. Not to believe him is not a sign of a broad tolerant mind, nor of a sophisticated intellect; it is the prime sin against intellect, since it is a fundamental sin against the God who made the intellect. And as for calling it tolerance, you might as well praise a man for tolerance for not trusting his wife too much or loving her too unreservedly. Not believing God is the basic and most virulent poison that has ever attacked the human personality, and has eaten the life out of it.

Look and live

'Nicodemus,' said Christ, 'do you recall the incident in the wilderness when Moses was commanded by God to make a serpent of copper and put it on a pole; then to erect the pole in a central position and bid everyone look at the serpent?' Yes, he remembered it well, for it is recorded in the book of Numbers.

It was one of those occasions in the wilderness when Israel had got lost. Not geographically lost: they still knew that if they made their way back in a south-westerly direction they would arrive back in Egypt. And similarly if they continued forward in a roughly northerly direction they would come to Canaan. But they were lost all the same, for they had begun the journey across the desert under the impression that it was not just a geographical journey. Thousands of tribes in those days migrated from place to place somewhat aimlessly, just pushed on by other tribes coming behind or drawn by the hope of new and better pastures. Israel had dared to believe their journey was not just a wandering; it was a journey led by God to the land that God had promised them.

But on the way they came to doubt God, to doubt his love, to question his wisdom, and in the end his very existence, which meant that the whole nature of their journey was now called into question. Was it a God-directed pilgrimage to a divinely appointed goal? Or was it simply a wandering through the wilderness? Why had they ever left Egypt to come on this crazy expedition anyway? In this situation doubt and unbelief were not clever variations on alternative theological schemes; they were a poison that was infecting the whole nation, sapping its morale and leading to disaster. They must be made to realize the seriousness of it. Suiting the punishment to the crime, God sent fiery serpents among them; and bitten by their poisoned fangs many died. If they could not be restored to faith, disaster faced the whole nation. It was then that God gave his strange command and a serpent of copper was erected on a pole. The cry went out throughout the camp that the people were simply to look to the serpent, and those who looked recovered and lived (Num 21).

The journey of life

The story about the fiery serpents is interesting because in a sense life for all of us is a journey. The question is, what kind of a journey? The Bible says that there is a promised land ahead; but multitudes have lost all faith in there being any promised land because they have lost or never had any personal faith in the God of the promised land. They have become cynical over life—just get the best grass you can in this sparse desert, and when the end comes, well, that's that.

But Nicodemus was listening, fascinated. The young prophet knew his Scriptures, but what was he implying now? Yes, it was a part of the inspired record that their forefathers, a long time ago, had sinned and come perilously near to perishing completely in the wilderness and never getting into the promised land at all. Was he suggesting that he, Nicodemus, was such a sinner that he was likewise in danger of never getting into the kingdom of God? Surely not! He was a sinner of course—everybody was; but not such a sinner surely, as to raise serious doubts as to whether he would ever get into the kingdom of God at all. Yes, Jesus had said earlier, 'Truly, truly, I say to you, unless one is born again he cannot see the kingdom of God.' But did he mean it in the absolute sense?

'Look here,' says Nicodemus to himself, 'I know I cannot say that I have at any time been born again, as he puts it. But surely that doesn't mean that I am in process of perishing, as he seems to suggest?'

Nicodemus had never thought of it before. He had always taken his theology seriously; but somehow being a professional theologian had hidden from him how immeasurably important true theology is. Being a theologian had somehow managed to make him feel that, if not perfect, he was well set for anything there might be in the way of heaven and the kingdom of God, or whatever you call it. As though being a doctor and knowing about medicine somehow meant that you could not possibly be ill or die. How difficult this young prophet had suddenly made it all appear. Unregenerate, unbeliever, and now a sinner in process of perishing, it was all too much. He had always done his best: how could he fairly be expected to do anything more?

'Nicodemus,' said Christ, 'isn't that story remarkable for the way in which God saved the people from perishing? It was not much that he asked them to do, was it? They could not have done very much anyway. Raging fever and incipient paralysis had reduced them to helplessness—they only had to look to the serpent of copper lifted up on the pole. They did not even have to understand just how that would help them or how the process worked—all they had to do was to look. And some in their sheer desperation did look, and were immediately healed and started to live again. Nicodemus, that story is a prophecy, as well as being a bit of ancient history. If you are to be saved, you too must be brought to believe. The problem is how. You can't make yourself believe, but believe you must, or you will perish.

'And therefore God has begun to do something about your desperate need. The Son of Man has already come down from heaven. Soon he must be lifted up as that serpent was, so that whoever believes may in him have eternal life. He will take the vast problem of the world's sin and unbelief and suffer its penalties and consequences to the full until there is no poison left, so to speak—any more than there was any poison in that serpent of copper after it had been through the fire. All who believe will be given new life in him, they will share the new life that he has made possible—and believing is not the hard thing that you think it is. You will find it simply a matter of taking your eyes off yourself, your efforts and attainments, and looking solely to the Son of Man as he is lifted up. Do as you are told, Nicodemus. Look to the Son of Man lifted up for you; and as you look you will find faith rising in your heart' (see John 3:14–15).

New birth and new sight

Soon after that the conversation ended, though exactly where it stops in the text it is not now possible to be sure. In 3:16–21 John has been led to add a number of explanations. Some of them Christ may well have used during his conversation with Nicodemus. Some of them were added for our sake (in the light of Christ's death, resurrection and ascension) to clarify some of the expressions that Nicodemus could not have fully understood before the cross, but which he came to understand immediately after that event.

For he did come to faith: the distinguished theologian was eventually born again. That much at least we can gather from what he did after Christ was crucified, along with Joseph of Arimathea, who likewise was a member of the Sanhedrin. Joseph had not consented to their deed, but when he saw Christ crucified, then he plucked up courage and took his stand and went to Pilate and asked for the body of Jesus (Luke 23:50–52). Together, he and Nicodemus prepared and buried Christ's body (John 19:38–42).

What a theologian he must have become after his new birth! His basic difficulty before had been that his theology had been nothing more than theology: it had been simply a philosophy for the head, not an introduction to a God who loved him personally and was seeking him and wanted him to trust him in a personal way. God in those days had been so remote, more like a series of propositions, or a mathematical formula. But then came the day when he saw the Son of Man lifted up on the cross, and he had looked. Suddenly the realization of what it all meant must have struck him. That real, living person on that cross was the Son of God, and he did not deserve to die like that. Nicodemus knew enough about him by that time to believe he was utterly innocent. Then why was he there? Was it that God just did not care? And then it dawned on him with overwhelming light and illumination. No! He was on that cross because God did care. He was writhing in pain under the penalty of Nicodemus' sin, the very sin that had poisoned Nicodemus' mind and destroyed what faith he had in God up to that point. He was on that cross but loving Nicodemus still, and suffering to bring him to faith. And the realization must have swept Nicodemus off his feet and drawn his heart out to Christ. He did not even have to try to believe. He believed; for beyond doubt this was God at work. God who so loved the world that he gave his only begotten Son that whoever believes in him should not perish but have eternal life (3:16).

He thought back to that first night and to his conversation with Christ. How wrong some of his impressions had been. As Christ had implied that he was an unregenerate man, and told him he was an unbeliever, and finally warned him that he was perishing, it had seemed that Christ was doing nothing but criticizing him at every turn and pessimistically condemning him. He was not, of course; any more than a doctor who diagnoses that a man has cancer is criticizing the man. It was only the first necessary and loving step in the process of exposing the trouble so that it might be cured. It was obvious now as he looked at his cross. Clearly God had not sent his Son into the world to condemn the world, but that the world through him should be saved (3:17). This was wonderful. To think that he, Nicodemus, would never now be condemned, and that he could be sure of it, beyond any doubt.

It was all so logical. How strange to think that, when Christ had at first kept insisting on belief and faith, it had seemed to Nicodemus that faith was arbitrary: something you had to make yourself do, even flying in the face of reason and understanding in order to do it. But now, when he saw what God was like and what God's love had done for him in Christ, he did not find it difficult to believe, any more than a child finds it difficult to trust the mother who holds her in her arms. Of course he was saved! God loved him; Christ had died for him to bear his sin and condemnation. Would that same Christ turn round one day and condemn him after all? It was absurd even to contemplate the possibility. Or if he did, one look again at the Christ on the cross would be enough to dispel any lingering doubt. 'Whoever believes in him is not condemned' (3:18).

The corollary is equally logical. At the time, he had thought Christ severe for saying that unbelievers were perishing; but how could it be otherwise? He had come to realize that Christ is the only begotten Son of God and not just a rabbi. Nicodemus may have thought, 'And just to think that's what I called him when we first met!' But he is not just a teacher come to prepare us to sit our final examinations on the day of judgment. Christ is himself the final examination; beyond him there are no other exams to be faced. He is God incarnate. Trust him and his love, and you have passed. Refuse to trust him, and, whatever else you go on to do, you have failed. 'Whoever believes in him is not condemned, but whoever does not believe is condemned already, because he has not believed in the name of the only Son of God' (3:18).

The problems still to be faced

There was a problem. What about all his colleagues in the theological schools? A decent bunch they were, and sincere most of them, as he had been himself. Moreover, they worked hard at their theology and he knew that some of them quietly gave quite a bit of money to the poor and did other excellent deeds. Did all these good works count utterly for nothing? And what about all the thousands of people who had not yet heard of Christ? Yes, there was a problem there. But there was an answer too. God's judgment is this: 'the light has come into the world, and people loved the darkness rather than the light because their works were evil' (3:19).

That is not to say that every person would be like this. Those who hear of Christ and then refuse to come to him, show by that refusal the real nature of their works, whatever their outward appearance may be. Their works are evil, done in unbelief and independence of God. Christ is God incarnate, and when those whose works are done genuinely to please God hear of Christ, they will come to him and trust him. He is the touchstone.

God of course knows the attitude of heart of every person who has never seen or heard of Christ. It was not necessary for Christ to come into the world in order for God to know that, but it was necessary for another reason. It was necessary if we humans were going to be able to have the final criterion available for our own use so that we could know where we stand long before the day of judgment. And the final criterion is what we do with Christ who is the light.

> For everyone who does wicked things hates the light and does not come to the light, lest his works should be exposed [or, reproved]. But whoever does what is true comes to the light, so that it may be clearly seen that his works have been carried out in God. (vv. 20–21)

Yes, there were problems. Faith had not done away with the need for theologians: men and women who could think through what God had done in Christ and what the Holy Spirit was saying about it. Nicodemus would not be out of a job. But thinking about a God you know personally, and pondering the statements of a God you are sure loves you—and all the world—well, it was altogether a different kind of theology from what he had tried to do before. He was in the kingdom of God now, and he could see it. And it is always easier to study something that you can see.

From Religious Bigotry *to* the Messiah

Now when Jesus learned that the Pharisees had heard that Jesus was making and baptizing more disciples than John (although Jesus himself did not baptize, but only his disciples), he left Judea and departed again for Galilee.

And he had to pass through Samaria. So he came to a town of Samaria called Sychar, near the field that Jacob had given to his son Joseph. Jacob's well was there; so Jesus, wearied as he was from his journey, was sitting beside the well. It was about the sixth hour.

A woman from Samaria came to draw water. Jesus said to her, 'Give me a drink.' (For his disciples had gone away into the city to buy food.)

The Samaritan woman said to him, 'How is it that you, a Jew, ask for a drink from me, a woman of Samaria?' (For Jews have no dealings with Samaritans.)

Jesus answered her, 'If you knew the gift of God, and who it is that is saying to you, "Give me a drink", you would have asked him, and he would have given you living water.'

The woman said to him, 'Sir, you have nothing to draw water with, and the well is deep. Where do you get that living water? Are you greater than our father Jacob? He gave us the well and drank from it himself, as did his sons and his livestock.'

Jesus said to her, 'Everyone who drinks of this water will be thirsty again, but whoever drinks of the water that I will give him will never be thirsty again. The water that I will give him will become in him a spring of water welling up to eternal life.'

The woman said to him, 'Sir, give me this water, so that I will not be thirsty or have to come here to draw water.'

Jesus said to her, 'Go, call your husband, and come here.'

The woman answered him, 'I have no husband.'

Jesus said to her, 'You are right in saying, "I have no husband"; for you have had five husbands, and the one you now have is not your husband. What you have said is true.'

The woman said to him, 'Sir, I perceive that you are a prophet. Our fathers worshipped on this mountain, but you say that in Jerusalem is the place where people ought to worship.

Jesus said to her, 'Woman, believe me, the hour is coming when neither on this mountain nor in Jerusalem will you worship the Father. You worship what you do not know; we worship what we know, for salvation is from the Jews. But the hour is coming, and is now here, when the true worshippers will worship the Father in spirit and truth, for the Father is seeking such people to worship him. God is spirit, and those who worship him must worship in spirit and truth.'

The woman said to him, 'I know that Messiah is coming (he who is called Christ). When he comes, he will tell us all things.'

Jesus said to her, 'I who speak to you am he.'

Just then his disciples came back. They marvelled that he was talking with a woman, but no one said, 'What do you seek?' or, 'Why are you talking with her?'

So the woman left her water jar and went away into town and said to the people, 'Come, see a man who told me all that I ever did. Can this be the Christ?' They went out of the town and were coming to him.

John 4:1–30

Ungodly religious hatred

There is no hatred so fiendish as religious hatred, nor any scandal so grievous as when people who profess to worship the same God and believe the same Bible live in open hostility to each other on the grounds of their religion. Yet that is how it was with Jews and Samaritans in the time of our Lord. The Jews worshipped Yahweh; the Samaritans professed to do the same. The Samaritans accepted the five books of Moses as the inspired word of God; so did the Jews. And yet for hundreds of years, except for a few brief periods when animosity died down a little, they lived in implacable hatred towards each other.

As is usual in cases like this, the trouble was rooted in the religious and political history of past centuries. According to 2 Kings 17:22–41, when the Assyrians deported the ten tribes of Israel, they filled Samaria with settlers from Babylon and the surrounding cities. These people had then been taught by an Israelite priest to worship Yahweh, but the worship of Yahweh as they practised it was horribly mixed up with the worship of the gods of their own native pagan religions: 'They feared the LORD and also served their own gods', as the historian puts it (see v. 41).

After the return of the exiles from Babylon, the Samaritans opposed the building of the temple and the wall of Jerusalem (Ezra 4:7–16), and eventually, in straight disobedience to the Scriptures, built themselves a temple on Mount Gerizim. It is understandable that the Jews did not like them. But the Jews, if technically correct, were no less bigoted; and so bitter did the rivalry between the two shrines become that around 129 BC the Jewish King John Hyrcanus captured the city of Shechem and destroyed the Samaritan temple. That merely stoked the fires of bigotry still hotter.

Round about the years AD 6–9 we hear of another outrage, this time perpetrated by the Samaritans against the Jews, though in retaliation for what we are not told. During the night they scattered human bones in the temple porches and all over the sanctuary.[1] For people who believed that dead bones carry ceremonial defilement, it was an act of appalling desecration. Later still we learn that in

---

[1] See Josephus, *Antiquities* 18.29.

AD 52 some Jewish pilgrims from Galilee who were going up to Jerusalem to celebrate a religious festival were attacked by Samaritans on the Samaritan border and one or more of them were killed. The Jews then retaliated by a revenge attack on some Samaritan villages.[2]

In religious belief and observance, the Samaritans differed from the Jews (in addition to their veneration of the holy place on Mount Gerizim) in not accepting any of the Old Testament beyond the Pentateuch. They were scrupulous in their observance of the Pentateuch, other than in the matter of the ceremonies connected with the Jewish temple, and they attached great importance to their claim that they were descended from the Jewish patriarchs, which the Jews denied. In all things to do with religious observance the Jews counted the Samaritans as Gentiles, and regarded them as impure from the very cradle onwards, and as causing impurity. That meant, among other things, that a Jew would not use the same utensils as Samaritans for cooking and eating, and generally speaking would have as few dealings as possible with them.

Moreover, even when things looked quiet, it took very little to arouse the rancour against Samaritans that lay beneath the Jewish skin. On one occasion, when our Lord and his disciples were refused lodging in a Samaritan village because they were on their way to Jerusalem, two apostles responded with the absurdly exaggerated suggestion that they should call down fire from heaven on the village (Luke 9:51–56). Christ rebuked his disciples for their fanaticism and, quietly accepting the peevish slight of the Samaritans, went on to another village to find lodging.

The name 'Samaritan' was one of the most offensive and insulting epithets a Jew could hurl against another Jew. When Christ once said something that pricked, they lashed back angrily at him: 'Are we not right in saying that you are a Samaritan and have a demon?' (John 8:48).

It is all a very sorry story, and not made any happier by the fact that the same bigoted and fanatical hatred has since shown itself a thousand times and more in Christendom. From it all there is one lesson that stands out clearly. Even if it uses the name of God or Christ, and busies itself with Jewish or Christian sacraments and

---

2   See Josephus, *Jewish War* 2.232–46; *Antiquities* 20.118–36.

symbols, religion is no more a sign that its devotees are regenerate than politics or commerce are signs that those who engage in those activities are regenerate. Some politics are conducted honourably enough and stem from the highest of motives; some politics are filthy. But the fact that a person engages in politics, even of the better sort, is no sign that he or she is necessarily regenerate. And the same applies to religion. All people are not by nature saints, but all people are by nature religious. The wildest and most murderous head-hunter is generally religious, and devoutly seeks the aid of his gods before going to poison his enemy or murder the neighbouring tribesmen in their beds. His religious devotion is no sign that the man is regenerate. Constantine the Great, before he confessed conversion to Christianity, slaughtered his enemies in the name of his pagan gods. His so-called conversion meant that he went on slaughtering his enemies, only now in the name of Christ. There was remarkably little evidence of regeneration in that either, but a great deal of misunderstanding, and consequently of misrepresentation, of what true Christianity is. And the saddest thing of all is that for many people this misrepresentation is the only kind of Christianity they know. When life goes well with them, they are glad to do without it; when life goes ill, it has nothing to offer them anyway. And they reject the whole thing out of hand. How difficult it is to get them even to consider that there might be something better. But, difficult as it is, it can be done. Let us watch how the Master himself did it.

Christ chose Samaria

When Christ left Judaea for Galilee he chose to travel via Samaria. The text says he had to (4:4); but the necessity was not geographical, for he could have crossed the Jordan down south, travelled up the east side of the river and crossed back again north of Samaria. The necessity must have lain elsewhere. It lay in fact in his love for the Samaritans. They were his creatures as much as the Jews. Some of them had been hurt by life; all of them needed salvation. Their religious zeal and tenacious clinging to tradition could not bring them peace with God nor satisfaction in their worship of him.

All of them needed to know of the gift of God, to discover what it means to worship the Father in spirit and in truth. The question was, how could Christ reach them and get to their hearts? It was useless to start by standing in their public square and preaching; a Jewish preacher would have been given very short shrift in Samaria. And so, with the ingenuity and tact of love, he found another way.

The woman who came to the well

It was high noon when he arrived in Sychar, and being tired after his journey he sat down by the well. It was scorchingly hot, and there were very few people about. The disciples had gone off to get food, and while a few shepherds might at this hour of the day come and water their flocks (see Gen 29:7), the women of the village would not be coming to draw water until the worst heat of the day was over.

Presently there came footsteps. He had been waiting to hear them, and knew why they came at this unusual hour. This woman's life had been sad and dissatisfying. She had had five husbands, and the man she now had was not her husband. We are not told why there had been so many husbands. Death may have taken some. Divorce in those days was all too easy for the man, and it may have removed others. But her craving for companionship and her longing for satisfaction were overwhelming. She had to have someone, even if he was not her husband. Perhaps this man was already married to someone else and they were really living in adultery. Or perhaps, while she craved for companionship, she was afraid this time to let her roots go down too deeply, and she shrank from the bond of marriage that had so often and so rudely been broken.

Yet living with a man who was not her husband was an unsatisfactory affair; it gave her no emotional security. All it did was to cut off all her friends. Now, whenever she came down the street, somehow everyone managed to be looking the other way until she had passed by; then she could feel their eyes following her. If she came to the well when the other women were there, they would move away without speaking and stand by in little groups until she had gone. She sensed what they were whispering under their breath. She had to come to the well, of course: thirst could not be denied its satisfaction, and water is one of life's necessities. But she preferred to keep away from people as much as she could, and that is why she was coming at this deserted hour.

She was taken aback a little when she saw a man sitting by the well; but he was not one of the local men. As far as she could see he was a complete stranger to those parts, and a Jew. He wouldn't know who she was or anything about her, so she reached the well and began drawing water.

But he knew. There was nothing he did not know about her. He knew her longings and cravings; he knew the bitter disappointments and disillusionment; he knew how life had mocked her. And what is more, he knew that, in spite of all her Samaritan tradition, religion had proved hollow and empty, unhelpful and utterly unsatisfying. But given her present ideas on what religion was all about it would be difficult to see how religion could possibly have healed her wounds or satisfied her heart. He must find a way of bypassing her religion and getting to her heart. If he could satisfy her at that level, the transformation in her life would be so evident that the whole Samaritan community would become aware of it, and perhaps many of them would seek the same satisfaction for themselves. How then could he get to her heart?

Opening the conversation

It was now a little past noon, and the stones round the well where he was sitting were baking hot like an oven. He was very thirsty, and the thirst was no accident. He had come a long way to meet this woman, a long way indeed when we remember who he was. The distance from being the Word who was in the beginning with God to being the Word made flesh who could feel thirsty after a morning's walk, was a distance immeasurable. But the distance had been covered, and now this was to be the meeting place between this deeply dissatisfied woman and God.

Because they both were human, she and Jesus shared a common, basic, physical thirst.

He waited for her to fill her pitcher. 'I wonder if you would give me a drink', he said.

The woman looked up and gasped with amazement. 'But you're a Jew. What are you doing asking for a drink from me when I'm a Samaritan?'

No Jew would normally have asked her for a drink, however thirsty he was. It would have been driven deep into his mind by his rabbinical teachers that Samaritan women were in a permanent state of defilement, and that any food or drink they touched was defiled and defiling. It was nonsense of course, for the Samaritan women were just as particular about keeping the Mosaic laws of hygiene as the Jewish women were. This cruel and wicked nonsense had burned deeply into the hearts of Samaritan women a sense of injustice at being socially rejected as if they were personally filthy. But that was religion, and she had come to take it for granted.

Was this Jew really asking her for a drink of water? It was too astounding to take in, and in her astonishment she apparently gave him none. He did not mind, for with his request he had got past the wall that for centuries had divided Jew from Samaritan. Her very astonishment showed it. And dimly, perhaps without her consciously being aware of it, the sense that she was respected as a human being, and that she was needed, had begun to register in her heart. In expressing surprise that he should ask water from her, she had made it so easy and natural for him to reply without giving offence that he was sorry that she had not asked water from him. 'If you knew the gift of God,' he answered, 'and who it is that is saying to you, "Give me a drink", you would have asked him, and he would have given you living water' (John 4:10).

The gift of God

Of course she did not know the gift of God, and he did not expect her to. She did not even know who he was, let alone what this gift of God was that he was talking about. She probably felt that God had given her remarkably little in her life except disappointment and sorrow, and as far as religion went, it seemed to her that it was more concerned with what she had to give God. If you wanted a priest to pray for you, you had to pay him. When you sinned and needed forgiveness, you had to pay for that too with a sacrifice. You had to tithe and pay regular dues. And even when you had paid everything they asked, no one was prepared to give you any assurance that you would definitely be saved. She had never heard that the heart of true religion is not what we give God but what he gives us; that there is a gift of God to be had simply for the asking, free and for nothing, but a gift without which it is impossible to worship God satisfactorily.

There are still millions like her. Perhaps they have never read the words of the New Testament: 'For by grace you have been saved through faith. And this is not your own doing; it is the gift of God, not a result of works, so that no one may boast' (Eph 2:8–9). Or even when they do read them, perhaps the concept is so foreign they do not take it in that salvation is a gift to be received. They think that it is something to be deserved and paid for, at least in the currency of good behaviour.

Still, you might have expected the woman to have said, 'Gift? Has God really got something he wants to give me? I didn't know. But if he has, then give it to me, please.' But no, she didn't. Like so many others, she heard the words, 'you would have asked him, and he would have given you living water', but it did not occur to her that this was an invitation to ask for the living water there and then. Besides that, she was puzzled by the term *living water*.

'Sir,' she said, 'you have nothing to draw water with, and the well is deep. Where do you get that living water? Are you greater than our father Jacob? He gave us the well and drank from it himself, as did his sons and his livestock' (John 4:11–12).

So the well was deep, and he apparently had nothing to draw the water with. If only she had known he didn't need her bucket. He could have done a miracle and quenched his thirst without rope or bucket or even a well. It was herself, not her rope and bucket, that he needed. Had it not been so, he need never have become physically thirsty. The physical thirst was but the result of a far deeper and more wonderful thirst: the need of God for his creatures. That is why he had waited for her to come, and why he had asked her to get the water for him. In a sense he had been waiting for her since time began.

It is not that the all-sufficient and all-satisfying God lacked something before we were created, and depended on us to fill some need. God is never driven by needs as we are; he never gets thirsty like we do. He never has to come to any well. And yet, by the deliberate choice of his sovereign will, he chose to need us. From the unfathomable deep of his infinite resources he made us, to satisfy the need he had chosen to have. While the human race stayed with him, all our wells were immeasurably deep and our thirst quenching resources infinite. But since we forsook him to go our own independent way, none of our wells has ever been more than pitifully shallow.

Our need for something deeper

'Living water?' she said. 'Where are you going to get living water from? Are you greater than our father Jacob who gave us this well?' The question was not meant to sound ludicrous. She probably took the term *living water* to mean *running water*, for in places such as Leviticus the term for running water is living water (14:6). And if he was not going to use water from the well, she could not see where he was going to get any running water from around there. And moreover, that well was to her something marvellous. She could not imagine why anyone should ask for any better water than it supplied. It not only went down deep into the earth, it also went back deep into history all the way to the patriarch Jacob. He was the greatest saint in the Samaritan religious galaxy, and to think that she was actually drinking water from the well out of which that great saint had once drunk made her feel good somehow.

What actual good it did her beyond quenching her thirst is difficult to see. She might regard the well as a holy well; but the water was nothing more than ordinary water. Jacob's *cattle*, as she herself remarked, had drunk of the well, with no noticeable effect on them beyond quenching their thirst. As a well of ordinary water, it was admittedly a tremendous social benefit, and Jacob had done a praiseworthy deed when he donated the well to the community. And let it be said, for it deserves to be, that in spite of all the scandals that can be told about religion, it is religion that has been at the forefront in providing social services and relief for the poor, the hungry and the ill. But although social relief is a valuable and necessary result of true religion, it does not lie at the heart of satisfying worship. We will need to go deeper than that.

Again the question was, how was he going to get across to this woman what the real living water is? All her life, religion for her had meant simply doing the material duties of life in the best way you could. It meant being a good mother to the children, being loyal to your husband, not telling lies, not gossiping too much, observing all the food laws and hygiene regulations taught by the priests from the Bible. And, like using your best china for special meals, it meant getting water, for drinking purposes at least, from the holy well of Jacob. How could she be brought to see the difference between religion at this level and the living water of a personal relationship with God at the deeper spiritual level?

> Jesus said to her, 'Everyone who drinks of this water will be thirsty again, but whoever drinks of the water that I will give him will never be thirsty again. The water that I will give him will become in him a spring of water welling up to eternal life.' (4:13–14)

He did not mean to imply that once a man or woman has had a taste of personal fellowship with God it so satisfies them that they never feel any desire to have another. Indeed, there is a sense in which once a person has tasted what it means to have fellowship with God it becomes the dominant desire of that person's life. He meant that once we have received the living water from Christ we have the source of satisfaction within us and are never again dependent on external sources of satisfaction, which, because they dry up, or are difficult to reach, or else are completely unattainable, leave us constantly dissatisfied. 'But the water that I will give him', Christ added to explain the reason why we would never thirst again, 'will become in him a spring of water welling up to eternal life.'

Living water indeed, because it was a life: the life of the Spirit of God, given by Christ to those who ask. Living water springing up from a spring within; not a feeling that comes stealing over us in church, or when we're admiring a splendid sunset, but a new life implanted within us and remaining there permanently. Living water that springs up naturally; not ecstatic emotions that have to be worked up or induced by a kind of Christian mantra. Living water from a spring that runs deep, its source being the very life of God, the life of eternity; a spring that therefore never runs dry, even in days of severe and lasting emotional drought, because it is basically not an emotional but a spiritual thing.

Obstacles to a relationship with God

A light came into the woman's eyes. She had seen something in what Christ had said that obviously attracted her and made sense. Was she about to ask him for the gift of God and receive it? 'Sir, give me this water,' she said, 'so that I don't get thirsty any more, and don't have to come all this way here to draw water.'

We heave a sigh of disappointment. Would she never understand that he was not talking about literal physical water? But Christ was not discouraged. She had sensed that there was something very attractive in what he said, and she had asked for it, even though she did not understand properly what it was. It gave him the opportunity of pointing out what was in fact not only the greatest obstacle to her receiving the living water, but also to her understanding what it is.

God is Spirit. True fellowship with him must therefore be at the level of spirit. Even to understand, let alone enjoy, the things of God one must first receive the Spirit of God (see 1 Cor 2:10–16). But it is precisely at this level that sin has blocked and broken all the channels of communication. How can one have fellowship with infinite holiness while sin is still unrepented of and unforgiven? How can you enjoy worshipping God if you are not certain that he has forgiven you, and are not sure whether in the end he will receive you or cast you into hell? Multitudes try to, as she likewise had tried to; but the whole thing was nothing but a wearisome duty. Living with a man who was not her husband had taught her that, however exciting and interesting it seemed to be at times, it was never satisfying. True love and fellowship even at the human level demand security. How can you admire and love a man if you are never sure whether at the end of the week you will still be his wife or whether he may by then have rejected and divorced you? Yet there are millions who try to love and worship God without being sure whether, when life ends, he will accept them into his heaven or banish them for ever.

Facing our true sinful identity

Until this woman had been made to face the fact that she was a sinner, until she had been brought to repentance and had received forgiveness and the assurance of the eternal security of God's acceptance, there was little she could know or understand about the living water of fellowship with God in the Holy Spirit. Yet to have faced her with her sin at the outset would have made her put up all of her psychological defences; made her feel that she was being criticized for not being good enough, and given her the impression (quite false, of course) that she was being told that she would have to be a great deal better before she could merit salvation. And if a Jew had told her, a Samaritan, that she was a sinner, she might well have slapped his face. But now she was interested in this living water, whatever it was, and had asked for it. Admittedly she did not yet understand what it was, and she was asking for the wrong reasons. Yet even the wrong reasons were understandable. The well at Sychar was a long way to have to come for ordinary water; and when life is going wrong emotionally and one is not in fellowship with God, the chores of life seem ten times the burden they are when one's spirit is free and glad. What if she could be brought to confess her status as a sinner herself? Forgiveness and salvation would make even the chores of life easier.

'So you would like this living water, would you?' said Christ. 'I tell you what; just go and call your husband, and come here.' Momentarily the woman hesitated; but then she recollected that he was a stranger and would know nothing about her. There was no need then to state the full facts and to get involved in long and embarrassing explanations. 'I have no husband', she replied. Strictly speaking it was true; but it was only half the truth. Really it was a cover up. But then who would want to expose a painful sore such as she had to the eyes of a perfect stranger? Yet half the truth could not do for Christ. He already knew the full truth. And if ever she was to be sure of the love of God and know security in her relationship with him, she would have to know that he knew it all. No use covering up and living in fear that one day he might find out the worst and reject her because of it.

So Christ must tear away the bandage and reveal the wound, and it was going to hurt. Notice with what infinite grace he did it. There was no open rebuke for not telling all the truth. Twice over he commended her for the fact that what she said was accurate, although she knew, and he was about to show that he knew too, that it was the nicely calculated accuracy of her phrase which she had hoped would cover up the full truth. 'You have expressed it quite well,' said Christ, 'in saying that you have no husband; for you have had five husbands and the man you now have is not your husband; it is exactly as you say.' There was no denunciation, no tirade against sin, no criticism. But the facts were there. Sandwiched between two commendations for accuracy, but there all the same: naked, bare, exposed, ugly and unpleasant.

Worship in spirit

The woman looked uncomfortable and confused. How did he know? Whatever could she say? He must be a prophet. No good trying any further cover up. Her mind was racing. A prophet meant religion. What could she say about religion to cover the embarrassment of the moment? Ah, he was a Jewish prophet. She knew what she could say to turn the pressure off herself a bit. 'Sir,' she said, 'I can see that you are a prophet. Our fathers worshipped in this mountain; and you say that in Jerusalem is the place where people ought to worship.' What a lot she could have gone on to say, if only he had started to argue the old controversy. She could have argued from the book of Genesis that Abraham had built an altar near there (12:7) and so had Jacob (33:20). She certainly could have shown, she felt, that the Samaritans were not so wrong as the Jews made out and that the Jews ought not to be so dogmatic, but ought to be prepared to let other people be right as well as themselves.

But there was no escape down the road of that old controversy. The Saviour was not prepared to argue the question. He could have shown her with divine clarity and force of argument that the Samaritans had been wrong all these centuries in opposing and refusing Jerusalem and clinging to Mount Gerizim. But how would it have helped her, even if he had won the argument and extorted from her a reluctant admission that he was right? For one thing, by the time the argument was finished, she would have attained her purpose of getting away from the question of her personal need and sin. And secondly, suppose he had proved that Jerusalem had been all the way along the right place to worship in—going to the right place, though important, had never even in those past centuries been the heart of the matter in true worship. Much less now, when even Jerusalem was going to reject its Messiah and God, and God was going to allow the Romans to destroy the temple in Jerusalem and move the question of worship on to an altogether higher plane. Yet he would not, even for the sake of winning this woman to faith, pander to the wrong ideas of Samaritan worship and pretend they were right, or else that it did not matter whether they were right or wrong. God had ordained that salvation should come via the Jews; and the Jew sitting there in front of her was her Saviour. It was important that she be reminded that she could not look in any direction she pleased for salvation. Salvation is a gift, but we can only have it from the Saviour God has provided. Jesus said to her,

> Woman, believe me, the hour is coming when neither on this
> mountain nor in Jerusalem will you worship the Father. You

worship what you do not know; we worship what we know, for salvation is from the Jews. But the hour is coming, and is now here, when the true worshippers will worship the Father in spirit and truth, for the Father is seeking such people to worship him. God is spirit, and those who worship him must worship in spirit and truth. (John 4:21–24)

She must have felt that things were beginning to close in on her. She had tried to get away from the subject of her own need and the unsatisfactory state of her own life before God by raising the question of worship. She had meant to discuss it at the impersonal level in terms of the historical and denominational controversy; and here the subject of worship, which she herself had raised, had brought her directly back to her own personal relationship to God. She could scarcely say now that she wasn't interested in the subject of worship. And what he was saying was so obviously right. Samaritans and Jews both believed that God is spirit; there was nothing she could dispute about that. And he wasn't saying the all-important thing about worship was the place you worshipped in, and that place must be Jerusalem. So she couldn't argue about that either. If God is spirit, it certainly sounded right to say his worshippers must worship him in spirit and in truth. But what exactly did it mean? And what did he mean by talking of true worshippers? Whatever he meant he seemed to infer that not all the Jews up in Jerusalem were necessarily true worshippers, which was some comfort to her at any rate. But she had never come across things put this way before. What did it all mean? She could not make it out.

But we have less excuse than she had for not knowing what it meant. He was not saying that all those who until this moment had worshipped in the temple in Jerusalem, or in Samaria for that matter, had been false worshippers in the sense that their worship had been hypocritical. But it had not, generally speaking, been the real full-blown ideal thing that is worthy of the name of *worship*.

A yachtsman may play at model yachts on the pond in the back garden with his six-year-old son in the hope that his boy will early on in life get interested in yachting, so that, when he grows up, he will join his father in sailing real yachts round the world. But if he's a yachtsman at all, or if he's a father at all, he could not be happy to see his son grown up to manhood and still content to play at model yachts on the garden pond. At that stage his father would want his son to go in for the real thing, or nothing.

Jewish symbols with the temple made of literal stone, and their Samaritan counterparts, were only intended as models pointing forward to the real thing. God is spirit: how could he forever remain satisfied with a puff of incense, some pretty coloured robes, and a woolly lamb as a sacrifice? He must have the real true thing. And the real true thing will be the thing that corresponds to the reality of his own nature: 'God is spirit, and those who worship him must worship him in spirit and in truth.'

At this point we cannot help remembering what our Lord told Nicodemus in his long conversation with him: 'That which is born of the flesh is flesh, and that which is born of the Spirit is spirit. Don't be surprised when I tell you, "You must be born again"' (see 3:6–7). To enter, or even to see, the kingdom of God we must be born again; not just improve, educate or religionize our flesh, but receive a new life of a different order by being born of the Spirit.

Now once more the same thing is being laid down in the area of worship. To worship God acceptably we must worship in spirit. That does not mean that when we go to church we should try to 'enter into the spirit of the thing', as people say. It means receiving the gift of God, the living water—the Holy Spirit, in fact—so that we can know and understand the things of God. It is impossibly unsatisfactory and unsatisfying to try to worship someone you do not really know; and Scripture points out that humans, apart from receiving God's Holy Spirit, have no means of knowing God.

> For who knows a person's thoughts except the spirit of that person, which is in him? So also no one comprehends the thoughts of God except the Spirit of God. . . . The natural person does not accept the things of the Spirit of God, for they are folly to him, and he is not able to understand them because they are spiritually discerned. (1 Cor 2:11–14)

Knowing God

It is important that we try to grasp what this means, for we can easily deceive ourselves here. We can enjoy the grandeur of a sunset, the colour of a butterfly's wings, the ecstasy of music; and because we recognize that all these and similar things are the good gifts of the Creator, we may think that this is what Scripture means when it talks about knowing God. But that is not so. We may know a lot about God at certain levels without knowing God.

Let us take an analogy. We have much in common with dogs and they with us. We enjoy a good walk, so do they. We like beefsteaks, they like beefsteaks. If your dog sees you eating a beefsteak, his interest is immediately aroused. He has a good idea of the gorgeous feelings that are at that moment tickling your palate and stomach, for he too has a stomach and a palate that understand beefsteaks. But the dog would be a very foolish dog if he imagined that, just because he could enjoy a beefsteak, he knew all about you. Take him into your study and show him your favourite oil painting, and at once he is lost. He cannot see anything in this curious object that you seem to be getting all excited about. He may bark if he sees you getting very worked up, but you shouldn't imagine it means that he has seen anything in the picture. Presently he will give the whole game away by trying to smell the picture; and when that does not yield any sensible result, he will try licking it. In the end, not making head or tail of it, he will get bored and give up on it completely.

However much you try to teach him to do little human tricks like sitting up or shaking hands, he will never understand the interest humans have in pictures nor in a thousand and one other human things. Vast areas of your personality are forever unknown territory to the dog. He will never know you in the full sense of that word, unless the impossible happens and you devise some way of imparting to your dog your human spirit.

And so it is with us and God. Enjoyment of God's handiwork in nature, enjoyment of human affection and genius, will tell us a lot about our creator. But that is not knowing God in the scriptural sense of the term. For that we need to receive the Spirit of God. Without him, says Scripture itself, the things of God will appear foolishness.

Indeed, this is the reason why many who have been brought up to regular attendance at some Christian place of worship, either keep attending simply out of a sense of duty or decency, or else abandon it altogether. It is all such a frightful bore and makes no sense. If they manage to keep attending, they will clamour for the sermons to be less about the Bible and more about politics and social responsibility; for they understand topics of that sort, and they seem relevant. Jacob to them, as to the Samaritan woman, will seem to have reached the height of spiritual attainment when he gave the local village a new waterworks; but prayer and Bible-reading they will dismiss as irrelevant. It is very understandable. The real fault lies not with them, but with whoever it was that admitted them to membership of a Christian church and urged them to try and worship God without making sure that they had first received the gift of God and been born again.

How then do we receive this gift and on what terms? The example of an actual conversion will make it clear. Here is the Apostle Paul telling us what conversion to Christ meant for him and particularly how it revolutionized his worship.

> Look out for the dogs, look out for the evildoers, look out for those who mutilate the flesh. For we are the circumcision, who worship by the Spirit of God and glory in Christ Jesus and put no confidence in the flesh—though I myself have reason for confidence in the flesh also. If anyone else thinks he has reason for confidence in the flesh, I have more: circumcised on the eighth day, of the people of Israel, of the tribe of Benjamin, a Hebrew of Hebrews; as to the law, a Pharisee; as to zeal, a persecutor of the church; as to righteousness under the law, blameless. But whatever gain I had, I counted as loss for the sake of Christ. Indeed, I count everything as loss because of the surpassing worth of knowing Christ Jesus my Lord. For his sake I have suffered the loss of all things and count them as rubbish, in order that I may gain Christ and be found in him, not having a righteousness of my own that comes from the law, but that which comes through faith in Christ, the righteousness from God that depends on faith. (Phil 3:2–9)

Worship in truth

But there is another mistake with regard to worship that Christ's words will save us from. We are to worship not only in spirit, but in spirit and *truth*. God is not the projection of our psychological states nor of our intellectual concepts. He is a reality: the Great Reality, the Truth. And he has manifested himself and shown us the truth of what he is like by sending his Son, the Word of God, into our world, where he died as the Lamb of God to take away the sin of the world and rose again from the dead. Worship, in order to be true, must be a genuine response to this revealed truth.

There is a danger with some, of thinking that 'worshipping in spirit' means having ecstatic experiences that are unrelated to Christian doctrine and to the great facts of salvation. Indeed, some will take the words of Paul out of their context: 'the letter kills, but the Spirit gives life' (2 Cor 3:6), and misinterpret them to mean that, so long as a person is having 'spiritual experiences', doctrine does not matter. They may even say that serious reading of Holy Scripture is not necessary and that doctrine is a positive hindrance to 'spirituality'. That of course is a deception. Worship in the Spirit of God will always conform to the truth of God. A person who, for instance, professes to be worshipping in spirit, and yet rejects the doctrine of the blood and sacrifice of Christ, is not worshipping according to truth. He is not worshipping the reality that is God and the reality of the historical manifestation of God in the person and work of Jesus Christ. He is worshipping some concoction of his own imagination. By contrast, Jesus invites the woman to worship God as he really is.

> The hour is coming, and is now here, when the true worshippers will worship the Father in spirit and truth, for the Father is seeking such people to worship him. God is spirit, and those who worship him must worship in spirit and truth. (John 4:23–24)

The woman's response

It was noon when the conversation started, and how long they had been talking we are not told, for what we have is no more than a summary of what passed between Christ and the woman. Certain things, however, stand out prominently in the conversation: God has a gift of living water, which she could have if she asked for it; she must confess to her status as a sinner and repent; God is seeking her, longing for her to become one of his real worshippers. It was not a question of her fathers and their traditions, nor her denomination or religious buildings or practices: it was a question of her and her personal response to God.

There came at length a lull in the conversation while Christ waited for her to make her response. Would she now personally ask him for the living water and receive the gift of God? 'Ah well,' she said, after a pause, 'we can't be sure about these things can we, any of us, not now? Of course, I know that one day the Messiah is coming, and when he comes he will explain everything to us.'

Millions have said the same thing since; for it seems to be one of religion's fixations that you can know nothing for certain now. It even enshrines itself in some prayers. Having asked God for this and that and the other, they add, 'and at the end, everlasting life'. But why 'at the end', why not now? Eternal life is not some remote thing that perhaps we may obtain when this life is done. 'Eternal life', said Christ, 'is knowing the true God, and Jesus Christ whom he has sent into our world' (see 17:3). It means knowing them now in the sense of having a living personal relationship with them now. Yes, of course, the relationship having begun here on earth will continue for all eternity; but it must begin on earth if ever it is going to exist in eternity. Why else did Christ come into our world? Why else was he in Samaria sitting by the well talking to this woman at all, if, when all is said and done, the verdict must be, 'But of course we cannot know anything for certain in this life'?

So she said, 'I know that the Messiah is coming, and when he comes he will explain everything to us.' But even in this remark there was hope, for it seemed to imply that when Messiah did come and explain everything she would believe him. What if her eyes could be opened to see that Messiah had not only already come, but was this very moment sitting by her side talking to her, and that the words she had been listening to were Messiah's explanations? Suppose he said, 'I am the Messiah', would she be able to take it in? She had noticed that he was a Jew; it was the very first thing she had noticed. Would her old religious prejudices allow her to accept even the Messiah, if he was a Jew?

But the difficulty had been overcome already. Had he not troubled to come and seek her? Had he not, tired and thirsty with his travelling, asked her, to her great amazement, for a drink of water? And had he not spent all this time talking to her, a woman, when many a Jewish rabbi would have regarded it as a waste of time and beneath his dignity to discuss theology with a woman? And had he not spoken to her, knowing all about her, when even her fellow townswomen snubbed and avoided her? He could say it now, and he would say it in a way that would tug deeply at her heart. Jesus said to her, 'I *who am speaking to you* am Messiah.'

What did she say? We are not told. And how little can be told of what goes on in a human heart when for the first time a person wakes up to the fact that the words she hears, and has heard many times, or has read many times in Scripture, are the words of the living Christ who is standing before her heart, personally seeking and waiting for her personal response of faith.

But just at this point the disciples arrived back with the shopping. They were dying to know who the woman was, and what on earth Christ was doing talking to a woman anyway. Mercifully they had the sense not to intrude with any tactless questions, though they did not get much chance to; for the woman suddenly got up and went hurrying back to the village.

'Is that your water jar?' said one of the disciples to another. 'No,' he said, 'it must be that woman's.'

'Lord,' they chorused, 'that woman has gone and left her water jar.'

The woman's confession and witness

It was a very natural thing that the Samaritan woman did, when in the joy and wonder of her experience of Christ she forgot her water jar. She had come to the well, deeply dissatisfied with life, at an hour when she might avoid meeting her fellow townspeople. But Christ had told her of a well of living, permanently satisfying water that he could place within her: the satisfaction of having and enjoying eternal life here and now, through a personal spiritual relationship with God. And evidently the woman must have asked for and received that satisfaction. She did not say it in so many words, but actions speak louder. She suddenly got up, hurried off into the town, and went to the people there and urged them to come and meet Christ.

Obviously something had happened. When she came to the well, she was trying to avoid the townspeople; now she was seeking them out. She had avoided them because they disapproved of her irregular behaviour, and she was ashamed or resentful. Now she was admitting she had been wrong, and she said to her fellow townspeople, 'Come, see a man who told me everything I ever did.'

Everything? What our Lord had told her about her personal life was the very irregularity which her neighbours objected to. Yet what she would formerly have resented anyone criticizing, she was now admitting. Somehow the pain and resentment had gone. Confession of her wrong was now transformed by the wonder of having discovered a Saviour who had known all about it without being told. He had not excused or condemned her past life, rather he had made her face it. Yet he had made her feel that even while she was still a sinner God loved her and valued her. In the strength of her newly found relationship with God, confession was comparatively easy.

From Anxiety *to* Trust

A FATHER'S PRAYER
AND DELAYED EVIDENCE

So he came again to Cana in Galilee, where he had made the water wine. And at Capernaum there was an official whose son was ill. When this man heard that Jesus had come from Judea to Galilee, he went to him and asked him to come down and heal his son, for he was at the point of death.

So Jesus said to him, 'Unless you see signs and wonders you will not believe.'

The official said to him, 'Sir, come down before my child dies.'

Jesus said to him, 'Go; your son will live.'

The man believed the word that Jesus spoke to him and went on his way. As he was going down, his servants met him and told him that his son was recovering.

So he asked them the hour when he began to get better, and they said to him, 'Yesterday at the seventh hour the fever left him.'

The father knew that was the hour when Jesus had said to him, 'Your son will live.' And he himself believed, and all his household.

This was now the second sign that Jesus did when he had come from Judea to Galilee.

John 4:46–54

Finding Jesus

On returning to Galilee our Lord went to Cana, the town where he had earlier turned water into wine (John 2:1–11). It so happened that at that time the son of a royal official in Capernaum was ill and seemingly beyond hope of recovery. Hearing that Jesus had returned to Galilee from Judaea, the boy's father in desperation decided to go to him and ask him to come and heal his boy.

Cana was some twenty miles from Capernaum, and he rode hard. It would take him some time to get there, and when he arrived he had to find where Jesus was and then persuade him to come to Capernaum and do the healing. What if when he arrived Jesus was in the middle of preaching one of his long discourses to the crowds? There was nothing he could do about that. He would just have to wait until it was over before he could get near enough to ask him. And then there would be the problem of getting him to Capernaum. How long would that take? Could he ask Jesus to ride horseback? Or would he have to be carried on a portable chair the way some of the nobles were? What if Jesus insisted on walking the whole twenty miles back? That would take a full day at least. It was an agony to contemplate, for time was slipping away and any minute could be the boy's last.

Arriving in Cana he found Christ and pleadingly put the question to him: would he come down to Capernaum and heal his boy?

'The trouble with you people', said Christ, 'is that unless you see signs and wonders you will not believe.'

'Look,' said the distraught father, 'if you don't mind, let's not stand here discussing fine points of theology. My boy is desperately ill; he could die any minute. Please come down at once before anything happens.'

'My good man,' said Christ, 'you have misunderstood me. Your son lives. He is already healed; you can go home.'

'Healed?' said the man. 'Already?'

'Yes, healed already', said Christ. 'You asked me to heal him, didn't you? Well, I have healed him. At this very minute he is alive and well. You see, I do not have to come to Capernaum to heal your boy, and you should be grateful that I don't. If I had had to travel all that way and lay my hands on him before I could heal him, he could easily have died before I arrived. As it is, standing here I have healed him. What I was observing just now is that you now have a problem of faith. I am telling you that your boy is well and that you can go home; but you cannot *see* that he is well. All the evidence you have at this moment that your son is well is my bare word; and in the nature of things, you cannot have any other evidence until you get home and see for yourself that my word is true. The trouble with you, and the rest of the people around here, is that unless you *see* signs and wonders you are not prepared to believe; and that means that these next few hours are going to be difficult for you. I am not coming to Capernaum with you. I say that your son is already well, and there is no need for you to continue standing here pleading with me; you can go home.

'You have to make up your mind then. If you cannot take my word for it that he is well without seeing signs and wonders, your next few hours till you get home are going to be full of worry and anxiety. It won't alter the fact that your son is well, for I *have* healed him. But if on the journey home you want peace of mind, you will have to be prepared to trust my bare word without any further evidence. I could, of course, here and now do some signs and wonders in front of you that you could see. But what would that prove? It would only prove that I can do miracles if I want to; and that much you already believe, for, if you did not, you would never have left home and come to me with your request. To do fifty miracles here and now before your very eyes so that you could see them would not prove that I can do a miracle of healing at a distance of twenty miles, and still less would it prove that I have done such a miracle. I'm saying that I have done such a miracle and that your boy is well. It is already true and nothing will change it.

'Moreover, when you get home you will have visible evidence that it is true, and has been true from the moment I said it. But you can't have that visible evidence until you get there. In the meantime, then, if you want peace of mind on the way, you had better learn to trust my word without demanding further evidence, and, acting on it in faith, journey home.'

The father's decision

The official didn't know quite how to feel. The past hours had been filled with mounting anxiety and tension. It seemed an eternity since the boy took ill. They would have called in the doctor at once, the very best in the palace service. But the boy's condition had steadily deteriorated, and there had come the sickening moment when the doctors had pronounced the case hopeless. Frantic with worry, he would have talked it over with his wife. He had heard in town that Jesus had returned from Jerusalem, where he had done a lot of amazing miracles, and he was now in Cana. Should they now try Jesus themselves? It would mean him leaving the lad and travelling to Cana, and he didn't like leaving him. He felt that he was doing something, if he was only sitting by the bed and holding his hand. It was irrational, of course; it was not helping the child, and it seemed to be only a matter of time now. So they decided to try Jesus. He was their only hope.

Tearing himself away from the bed, he had ridden those twenty desperate miles as fast as he possibly could. Every mile covered had tortured him with the realization of what a long way he had to bring Jesus back before he got him home. From time to time hope would set his imagination running: he could see himself urging Jesus forward the last few steps into the house and then into the bedroom. He could picture the dramatic moment as Christ would lay his hands on the child's head and the little fellow would sit up and say, 'I feel better now, Dad.'

Then the horse would stumble a bit and the official would come back to reality. He had not reached Cana yet, let alone got back again. Still more miles to go. Would he never get there? By the time he reached Christ, he had already worked out what method he would suggest to Christ for getting him to Capernaum as fast as ever possible, if only he was willing to come, the exact route they should follow, and the time it would take.

And now suddenly there was this strange anti-climax. 'The boy', said Christ, 'is already well.' It was difficult to know how to feel. There was no sense of any miraculous power surging around, no electrified atmosphere about him, no ecstatic exultant feelings within him; nothing except the simple plain statement of Christ, 'Go, your child lives.' After all the stress and anxious excitement, it seemed unreal.

Nothing but a bare word! Had he got to be content with that, when every nerve and blood vessel in his body was tensed to its limit and crying out for action? A bare word: dare he stake his child's life simply on what this man said, without any further evidence? Christ had said, of course, that the matter was already settled and the child was already well. For Christ, it was not a question of risking whether the child would be saved or not, for he had already healed him the moment his father had asked him to come. The question for the father was, what if Christ was not true and his word could not be trusted? Then the child was not healed, and would die, perhaps even before he got back. But then, even without Christ, the child was going to die anyway. If Christ had not in fact healed him, it made no difference—except that Christ was now telling lies. And if Christ was palming him off with lies, there was no point in continuing to plead with a liar to come and heal his boy. On the other hand, if Christ was telling the truth he was already well and there was no need to continue pleading with Christ to come and heal him. Either way, he must go, and begin the journey home.

What should he believe? He had come staking his last hope on Christ's miraculous powers; but the question now was not his miraculous powers but his character. Was this Jesus to be trusted, or was he a deceiver? He must make up his mind. How would he do that? The sight of his little boy as he had last seen him rose before his mind. He could see his wife, her heart fit to break, anxiously trying to soothe him as he tossed in his delirium. 'Go,' said Christ, 'your son lives.' It was no good dithering: he must make up his mind about this Jesus, whether he should trust him or not, and then act upon it. As a palace official he was used to meeting men and having to decide whether to take them at their word or not. He must do the same with Christ. He turned and looked Christ straight in the face, man to man. For a long moment his eyes searched the eyes of Christ and scanned his countenance. John tells us, 'The man believed the word that Jesus spoke to him' (4:50). We can easily imagine that presently he said to him, 'Thank you, Lord. Thank you for healing my child', and with a deep bow he turned and walked away.

The return journey

It was only the seventh hour, or one o'clock in the afternoon, and that meant that if he had left at once and ridden back to Capernaum as hard as he had ridden to Cana, he could have reached Capernaum by dusk the same day. In actual fact the record tells us that he did not arrive back home until the next day (v. 52). Where he went and what he did in the meantime we are not told. We may be sure that it was no lack of love for his child or his wife that made him delay his return home. Perhaps it was the sleepless nights and the strain of the last few days, and the hectic ride to Cana that now led to a reaction, and he felt he just could not face the ride back until he had some sleep. But whatever he did, the delay in returning home is an excellent testimony to his faith. Christ had said that the boy was well, and the man believed what he said.

Faith meant not only giving reluctant and half-hearted consent to Christ's statement, but believing it and acting on its implications. If Christ said the boy was well, he was well. Probably by this time he was out of bed and starting to play with his toys. As for his wife, she would already be deliriously happy. The miraculous suddenness with which the boy had recovered would have already let her know that her husband had reached Christ and that it had been the power of Christ that had healed the boy. She would have a profound sense that all was well, so there was no need for him to go rushing back home as fast as he had come. True, he himself still had no evidence that this was what was happening at home, except for the bare word of Christ and what could be logically deduced from that word. But then true faith is—and is expected to be—logical (see Matt 16:5–12).

The next day, by the time he was getting near home, his servants had decided that he must soon be arriving and they came out along the road to meet him, all excited with the news that his son was perfectly well. 'As a matter of interest,' said the father, 'at what precise moment did the lad begin to get better?'

'Yesterday,' they said, 'at the seventh hour the fever suddenly left him.'

He thought for a moment. 'At the seventh hour yesterday', he said. 'Let me see—yes, that was the very time I had just found Christ and was asking him to come back home and heal the lad, and he said, "I don't need to, the boy is already well. I have now healed him".'

The way belief works

There come times in life when the distinctions of our human condition—distinctions of rank, time and distance—seem to fade away and for a moment eternity floods our spirits with a vivid sense of the immediacy of its unchanging realities. Such a moment occurred that morning on the Cana road just outside Capernaum, as master and servants together discovered the unchanging, timeless and universally present reality of the utter reliability of God in Christ. For the servants and the rest of the official's household, it was a question of believing Christ for the first time; but for the official himself it was the culmination of a process of increasing faith. Twice the Scripture explicitly mentions that 'he believed'. Verse 50 says, 'The man believed the word that Jesus spoke to him', while verse 53 says, 'And he himself believed, and all his household.'

Actually the first time he had believed was when he left home to go to Jesus. Before that, he had heard of Jesus and his ability to do miracles, and it had interested him in a vague sort of way, but he had never exercised any personal faith in Jesus or his power. When, however, he was faced with the reality that his child was going to die, Christ became his only hope. And it was then that he made his decision. He decided that there was nothing he could do by staying at home by the bedside: the only hope lay in going to Christ and asking him to come and heal the boy. He made his decision, and acted upon it. And he had no sooner asked Christ to heal the boy, than Christ healed him; for it is an unvarying principle that, 'everyone who calls on the name of the Lord will be saved.' And when he says that, the Apostle Paul first gives the reason: 'for the same Lord is Lord of all, bestowing his riches on all who call on him' (Rom 10:12–13).

Delayed evidence

Then there had to come the next, and probably more deliberate and conscious, act of faith. When he had first set out to seek Christ his faith was based on reasonable evidence: he had heard of all the miracles that Christ had done at Jerusalem at the feast (John 4:45), and in addition he had doubtless heard of the earlier miracle at Cana of Galilee. But when Christ said 'Go; your son will live', he had no evidence on which to base his faith. He evidently had never known of any case in which Christ had healed at a distance, for if he had, he would surely have asked Christ to heal his son at once without first travelling to Capernaum.

He was therefore faced with the challenge to believe the word of Christ without any evidence, save only the character of Christ. It was not that in this case the evidence was faulty. It lay in the nature of things; in the nature of time and space. In a time before any form of instant long-distance communication had been invented, the man could have no evidence that his son, twenty miles away in Capernaum, had been instantaneously healed. Later, when he got home, there would be evidence; but for the moment it was unavoidable: for him the evidence must be delayed. Yet the man believed and once more acted on that belief. And it was not irrational of him, for to his knowledge Christ had done many other miracles. While that did not prove he had now done this one as well, it was reasonable grounds for trusting until evidence became available. The irrational thing would have been to demand the evidence that this particular miracle had taken place, before it could possibly be available.

The evidence of salvation

His case is not without its lesson for us. When we come to Christ for salvation, we come with the evidence all around us of how he has saved thousands of other people. When we personally call on the name of the Lord he saves us instantaneously, 'for everyone who calls on the name of the Lord will be saved.' But the evidence that he has saved us, has given us eternal life, will make us holy, will bring us home to heaven at last, must in the very nature of things be more or less delayed. It will only come to light bit by bit as we go along, and it will not finally be complete until we reach heaven. But, having come to Christ and asked for salvation, we are required to take him at his word and, believing that same bare word, act upon it in faith and begin our journey home, allowing the evidence to disclose itself as we go along.

And it is to be observed that if, when Christ had said to the man, 'Go your way, your son lives', the man had not gone but had continued to pray that Christ would heal his boy, his continued praying would not have been a sign of faith, but a sign of unbelief. And serious unbelief, as John argues in his first letter (5:9–12). If God says: 'He that has the Son has life', and I say, 'I *have* received God's Son, but I am not sure if I have life or not, so I continue to pray that God will give me life'—*that* prayer is an insult to God. For if God says I have life, to then ask him to give me life, is to show that I don't believe what he says, and that is to make God out to be a liar.

Moreover, the inevitable absence of immediate evidence will drive us, as it drove the official, to place our faith in the character of Christ as a person, and not merely in the fact that he has done this or that work. There are of course many facts about the work and person of Christ in respect of which we are required to believe that such and such a fact is true. For instance, we are required to believe that Jesus is the Son of God (1 John 5:5); and very important it is too that we should believe the fact. But away and beyond the importance of believing these facts about Christ, is the importance of believing and trusting Christ himself as a person. And faith in him as a person will often lead us into situations when we are required to believe him without any immediate evidence, or even in spite of apparently contradictory evidence. But the evidence will always sooner or later be forthcoming, as surely as it was for the official when he reached home.

Believing more than once

When he eventually heard from his servants that his boy was well, and discovered that he had in fact recovered precisely at the hour in which Christ had said 'Go; your son will live', we read that 'he himself believed' (John 4:53). It obviously does not mean that he had not believed before, but now he believed in a somewhat different way. When he stood in Cana talking to Christ, he had decided to 'believe the word that Jesus spoke to him' (v. 50). It was largely a matter of the will; and while a man can control his will, he cannot completely control his emotions and feelings. He had decided to believe Christ's word; and logically deducing from that word that there was now no need for him to hurry home at once, he had apparently put up for the night in a hotel or a friend's house somewhere.

Perhaps when he woke up in the morning, if not before, his emotions suggested to him that the whole thing might be false, and he had had to take a grip on his determination to believe the word of Christ no matter what his emotions felt like. But when he got home and the evidence stared him in the face, it was no longer a question of the will, nor of deciding to believe. Belief was automatic. But if our own experience is any guide, belief this time was accompanied by a profound sense of awe at the utter reliability of Christ; the sense that Christ's word had been true right from the very start. His boy had been made well and nothing was going to change it, even if his own emotions were still making him feel afraid that the boy might not be well. It quite likely was accompanied by a feeling of shame that his emotions had ever suggested any fears and doubts; and a determination by God's grace never to doubt Christ's word again.

From Death *to* Hope

WHEN CHRIST CAME
TO RAISE LAZARUS

Now a certain man was ill, Lazarus of Bethany, the village of Mary and her sister Martha. It was Mary who anointed the Lord with ointment and wiped his feet with her hair, whose brother Lazarus was ill. So the sisters sent to him, saying, 'Lord, he whom you love is ill.'

But when Jesus heard it he said, 'This illness does not lead to death. It is for the glory of God, so that the Son of God may be glorified through it.' Now Jesus loved Martha and her sister and Lazarus. So, when he heard that Lazarus was ill, he stayed two days longer in the place where he was. Then after this he said to the disciples, 'Let us go to Judea again.'

The disciples said to him, 'Rabbi, the Jews were just now seeking to stone you, and are you going there again?'

Jesus answered, 'Are there not twelve hours in the day? If anyone walks in the day, he does not stumble, because he sees the light of this world. But if anyone walks in the night, he stumbles, because the light is not in him.'

After saying these things, he said to them, 'Our friend Lazarus has fallen asleep, but I go to awaken him.'

The disciples said to him, 'Lord, if he has fallen asleep, he will recover.' Now Jesus had spoken of his death, but they thought that he meant taking rest in sleep.

Then Jesus told them plainly, 'Lazarus has died, and for your sake I am glad that I was not there, so that you may believe. But let us go to him.'

So Thomas, called the Twin, said to his fellow disciples, 'Let us also go, that we may die with him.'

Now when Jesus came, he found that Lazarus had already been in the tomb four days. Bethany was near Jerusalem, about two miles off, and many of the Jews had come to Martha and Mary to console them concerning their brother. So when Martha heard that Jesus was coming, she went and met him, but Mary remained seated in the house.

Martha said to Jesus, 'Lord, if you had been here, my brother would not have died. But even now I know that whatever you ask from God, God will give you.' Jesus said to her, 'Your brother will rise again.'

Martha said to him, 'I know that he will rise again in the resurrection on the last day.'

Jesus said to her, 'I am the resurrection and the life. Whoever believes in me, though he die, yet shall he live, and everyone who lives and believes in me shall never die. Do you believe this?'

She said to him, 'Yes, Lord; I believe that you are the Christ, the Son of God, who is coming into the world.'

When she had said this, she went and called her sister Mary, saying in private, 'The Teacher is here and is calling for you.' And when she heard it, she rose quickly and went to him. Now Jesus had not yet come into the village, but was still in the place where Martha had met him. When the Jews who were with her in the house, consoling her, saw Mary rise quickly and go out, they followed her, supposing that she was going to the tomb to weep there.

Now when Mary came to where Jesus was and saw him, she fell at his feet, saying to him, 'Lord, if you had been here, my brother would not have died.'

When Jesus saw her weeping, and the Jews who had come with her also weeping, he was deeply moved in his spirit and greatly troubled. And he said, 'Where have you laid him?' They said to him, 'Lord, come and see.'

Jesus wept. So the Jews said, 'See how he loved him!'

But some of them said, 'Could not he who opened the eyes of the blind man also have kept this man from dying?'

Then Jesus, deeply moved again, came to the tomb. It was a cave, and a stone lay against it. Jesus said, 'Take away the stone.'

Martha, the sister of the dead man, said to him, 'Lord, by this time there will be an odour, for he has been dead four days.'

Jesus said to her, 'Did I not tell you that if you believed you would see the glory of God?'

So they took away the stone. And Jesus lifted up his eyes and said, 'Father, I thank you that you have heard me. I knew that you always hear me, but I said this on account of the people standing around, that they may believe that you sent me.'

When he had said these things, he cried out with a loud voice, 'Lazarus, come out.' The man who had died came out, his hands and feet bound with linen strips, and his face wrapped with a cloth.

Jesus said to them, 'Unbind him, and let him go.'

John 11:1–44

Six days before the Passover, Jesus therefore came to Bethany, where Lazarus was, whom Jesus had raised from the dead. So they gave a dinner for him there. Martha served, and Lazarus was one of those reclining with him at table. Mary therefore took a pound of expensive ointment made from pure nard, and anointed the feet of Jesus and wiped his feet with her hair. The house was filled with the fragrance of the perfume.

But Judas Iscariot, one of his disciples (he who was about to betray him), said, 'Why was this ointment not sold for three hundred denarii and given to the poor?' He said this, not because he cared about the poor, but because he was a thief, and having charge of the money bag he used to help himself to what was put into it.

Jesus said, 'Leave her alone, so that she may keep it for the day of my burial. For the poor you always have with you, but you do not always have me.'

John 12:1–8

A sign that was also a parable

John 11 records the final sign of a series of seven that were written, according to John, 'so that you may believe that Jesus is the Christ, the Son of God, and that by believing you may have life in his name' (20:31). So this miracle of the raising of Lazarus has that general function; but what specific function is it meant to have?

I suggest to you that one of the functions it was deliberately intended to have was a very practical one. Christ was going away. This is the start of what would be his final visit to Jerusalem. He would be crucified, buried, then raised again and ascend into heaven. Even the apostles, let alone those who had believed on him throughout the land, were not really expecting him to die. When eventually he said to them in the Upper Room, 'I'm going away, and sorrow has filled your heart because I say it', they could scarcely believe it even then. He had to tell them, 'It is expedient for you that I go away.' Chapters 13–17 tell us the reason that was so. His going away was essential for their sanctification, which depended upon the Holy Spirit's coming; and he would only come after Christ went away.

So he was going. What would happen all down those years when he was away? What was the programme? How would they continue to believe in him, in his love and care for them while he was away and the harsh realities of life, particularly death, rolled in like storms on the sea?

The matter is touched on right from the very beginning of chapter 11. This family from Bethany that we meet—Martha, Mary and Lazarus—was very much attached to the Lord. It was the same Mary who would anoint the Lord's feet with ointment (11:2; 12:3), which we will consider shortly. It was a family with whom Christ had stayed on occasions: witness Luke's record of it (10:38–42). When Lazarus grew sick, the two sisters sent a letter to our Lord saying, 'he whom you love is ill' (John 11:3). Notice the tact of the letter. It didn't say, 'Lazarus is sick. Please come as quickly as you can and get here!' No, you don't talk to friends like that, do you? It just informed him that Lazarus 'whom you love' is sick. They expected that the love our Lord had personally for them and for Lazarus would be enough to move him to come. But he didn't attempt to come. In fact, when he heard that Lazarus was sick, he stayed where he was for two more days (11:6).

Healing at a distance

If you think of the story of the palace official's son (4:46–54) that we thought of in our previous chapter, you might find this a little bit disconcerting. We recall the record of that miracle was that this man's son was sick and at the point of death, and he had come to our Lord to ask him to heal his son. He believed that Jesus could heal him, but Jesus had been down at the feast at Jerusalem and there was no way of contacting him. Then the man heard that he had come back up to Galilee. Now there was a chance! Jesus was in Cana of Galilee, so the official came from Capernaum down by the lake, and up over the hills to Cana and asked him to *come* and heal his son. And Jesus said to him, 'The trouble with you people around here is that unless you see signs and wonders, you will not believe.'

And the man, if I may paraphrase him, said, 'Lord, look, my son is desperately sick; don't stop here and talk theology. We can talk theology later on after he's better, but he's desperately sick. Please, if you don't mind, *come* at once! Lay your hands on him!'

And our Lord said, 'My good man, you have misunderstood me. Your son is already better.'

'My son is already better?'

'Yes. You asked me to heal him, didn't you? I've healed him.'

That put the man on the spot, because he could not see that the boy was well! And now Christ was demonstrating a thing that we hadn't been told before in John: that he could heal at a distance. The man had to decide whether he would believe Christ or not. To his credit, he believed and got up and went home; though he didn't get home until the next day, apparently. It wasn't until he got home that he actually saw the evidence. Yes, the boy was well. And to satisfy his curiosity he said to the servants, 'But tell me now, just what hour did he begin to get better?'

And they said, 'Oh, it was yesterday about the seventh hour.'

He worked it out. It was at the very moment when (and this becomes important), 'when he believed'? No, it doesn't say that. It was at the moment 'when Jesus had *said* to him, "Your son will live"' (4:53).

It was a miracle that shows that Christ could heal at a distance. And if you have been listening to that miracle, you will say, 'Well, it's obvious what he's going to do in the case of his friend when he gets a note from Bethany that Lazarus, whom he loves, is desperately sick. He doesn't need to go. He can stay two days in the place where he was because he can heal at a distance! He'll just say the word and Lazarus will be healed. Simple, isn't it?'

But two days later he said to the apostles, 'Lazarus has fallen asleep.'

And they said, 'Oh, Lord, he'll do well if he's fallen asleep, because he'll recover.'

'No,' he said, 'what I mean is he's dead.' Then he added, 'I'm glad I wasn't there.'

What on earth is he saying? If he could heal at a distance he didn't need to go, but he could have healed him!

You might say to yourself, 'Oh well, he didn't heal him, but now he'll speak a word from a distance and raise him from the dead.'

He didn't do that either. Instead he said, 'Let's go to Judaea.'

Martha and Mary react

When he got to Bethany in Judaea, Martha came out to meet him. Her first words were, 'Lord, *if you had been here*, my brother would not have died' (11:21).

Our Lord responded, 'Your brother shall rise again.'

'I know that', said Martha. (She was a good Pharisee, in that sense. Like them, she believed in the resurrection.) 'I know he shall rise at the last day, Lord. But that's a bit irrelevant right now, isn't it? *If you had been here*, he wouldn't have died to start with!' What she was implying was, 'Why didn't you come?' Yet Martha's faith remained triumphant. She said, 'Lord, even now I believe that whatever you ask from God, he will give you.'

When Martha was done talking to Christ, Mary came out. She wasn't the theologian that Martha was. As she collapsed at his feet, all she could manage to get out were the words, 'Lord, *if you had been here*, my brother would not have died.'

Our Lord was moved when he saw her tears, and those of the other mourners. The crowd knew that he loved Lazarus, yet some of them said, 'He could heal a blind man. Why couldn't he have healed this man and kept him from dying? He was supposed to love him, wasn't he?' He groaned in spirit because now it raised the question of whether he really did love Lazarus.

The timing of the resurrection

Of course, we know that he did raise Lazarus from the dead. But that miracle of bringing him back was, like the other miracles, a *sign*. The multiplying of the loaves and fish, for instance, was a sign that Jesus is the bread of life (6:35). What do you suppose this miracle of raising Lazarus was a sign of? It was a sign, in the words he explicitly said to Martha, that Jesus is 'the resurrection and the life' (v. 25).

When is the resurrection going to take place? Is it going to happen every other day, or every other century? No, the resurrection will only happen when Christ comes back! He is not going to stage it in his absence. The rest of the New Testament insists on this point. The resurrection will take place at 'the *coming* of the Lord'. The resurrection of the believer will not take place in our Lord's absence. He will not sit on the throne of heaven and suddenly speak the word, and then all the dead will rise.

> *For the Lord himself will descend from heaven* with a cry of command, with the voice of an archangel, and with the sound of the trumpet of God. And the dead in Christ will rise first. Then we who are alive, who are left, will be caught up together with them in the clouds to meet the Lord in the air, and so we will always be with the Lord. (1 Thess 4:16–17)

> For as in Adam all die, so also in Christ shall all be made alive. But each in his own order: Christ the firstfruits, then *at his coming* those who belong to Christ. (1 Cor 15:22–23)

The raising of Lazarus is a sign of the great reality of the resurrection and the reuniting of the living and the dead when the Lord comes. And so we have the demonstration of Martha and Mary sending the letter to him, which said, 'He whom you love is sick.' It was a prayer for Lazarus' recovery, for healing from his sickness. And our Lord stayed away and let Lazarus die. But he then raised him when he came to them! What a simple parable that is, though it is also a miracle. It is put here to prepare the Lord's people for his going away after he was crucified, had risen from the dead and ascended back to heaven.

Those who have fallen asleep

What happens now, during this time when Christ is away, when his people's loved ones get sick? Well, we send a message to the Lord, don't we? 'Lord, dear brother so-and-so has been taken into hospital with a heart attack.' And if it pleases the Lord he will give him recovery, and often he does. But ultimately he doesn't, does he? Am I not right in saying that, since the Lord ascended to heaven, most believers have died? I'm not denying that sometimes the Lord answers our prayer and heals our loved ones when they are sick; he does do that. But ultimately, until the Lord comes, we shall all die.

There's no need to get upset about it. Look at the pattern. The dead will be raised and reunited with the living when the Lord *comes*.

This sign for Martha and Mary and Lazarus was also a parable for us so that we should not be disturbed when our Lord, in his absence, allows our loved ones to die. It holds out the promise of his second coming. He will come again! And it is delightful to see that he did come again after he had raised Lazarus.

> Jesus therefore six days before the Passover came to Bethany, where Lazarus was, whom Jesus raised from the dead. So they made him a supper there . . . (John 12:1–2 RV)

Allow your imagination to dwell upon that brief moment in history. Here were Martha and Mary, plus the disciples, plus the Lord, and Lazarus—now raised from the dead, and they made the Lord a supper! There shall come another supper, shall there not? When the dead are raised and the living changed, along with a host of the disciples of all the ages, there shall be a supper. It will be the Lamb's bridal supper (Rev 19:6–9).

So the sign in John 11 is meant to stand for the comfort and encouragement of every believer all down that age when our Lord is absent and does not yet come. This is our Lord setting the programme by this parable, by this miracle, so that we shall not be upset down through the years. He was preparing his people—Martha and Mary and Lazarus, and all who would follow—for his going away and his eventual coming again.

And yet, helpful though his preparation of his followers would prove to be, it was the fact that those who had come to believe in him were about to face his going away; and not only his absence, but first his death. For him to raise from the dead a close friend was marvellous, but what would it mean for all of their hope if the one who claimed to be the resurrection and the life himself died? Preparing his followers to face that challenge to their faith would require another lesson.

Prepared for his own burial

As far as God is concerned, death is a stain and defilement on his universe. Death is an insult to God the creator, a stench obnoxious to God. It was God who made humans in his own image, so a dead corpse going to corruption is as obnoxious to him, and more so, as it is to us. And in the Old Testament he taught his people that those who approach him must be cleansed from every stain and smell of death.[1]

As we journey through John's Gospel, we come to the time of the great Passover, and we see the people as they are going up to Jerusalem to purify themselves from the stain of death. All unknown to them, here comes the great Passover Lamb. By his death he shall remove every stain of sin and grant all who believe in him new life— life in Christ, the very life of God, a life that shall never die—and enable them to come to God in spirit and truth. They can approach into the very presence of the incorruptible and immortal God. That is the setting of these chapters. And they open with the scene that unfolded at the supper prepared for our Lord in the home of Mary, Martha and Lazarus in Bethany.

While they were gathered there, he announced that he was about to be buried. Far from being afraid to come to Jerusalem because he might die, he announced that he was going to be buried. Except maybe for Martha and Mary, that was news to his disciples. Though they had been told many times, they just couldn't get it into their heads that Jesus was going to die. Not until they actually saw him dead could they take it in. They thought that he was going to reign immediately as king. Yet here he was, before he came as king, announcing that he was going to die.

It was not only that he would die, but that he would be *buried*. When someone objected to Mary anointing his feet with expensive

---

1   See, for example, Lev 21.

ointment, Jesus said, 'Leave her alone, so that she may keep it for the day of my *burial*' (12:7). That is an important part of the gospel, for the gospel is that, 'Christ died for our sins in accordance with the Scriptures'; but also, 'that he was buried,' as literally as you or I might be one day, and 'that he was raised on the third day in accordance with the Scriptures' (1 Cor 15:3–4).

It was Judas who objected, and when he did, Jesus said, 'The poor you always have with you, but you do not always have me.' This was how he defended Mary's pouring of the ointment on him. She had given him an anointing with nard, worth more than three hundred denarii. In those days, a labourer got one denarius a day. Since they didn't work on the Sabbath, three hundred denarii would have been the yearly wage of a day-labourer. Let's put it in modern terms. She spent an entire year's wages on Christ all in one go! Christ's first justification for her action was that he was about to die and be buried.

Judas said it was irresponsible, and a sign of religion gone fanatical. It ought to have been sold and given to the poor! 'What kind of a testimony would it be to the world, if they were to see us wasting it when there are poor folks who haven't got enough money to buy the next crust of bread?' There are modern Judases who talk like that too. Of course, he was a thief, and if that nard had ever been sold, he was looking to pocket some of the interest, if not the capital, out of the proceeds of the sale.

If one of your family members, say a daughter, were to demand a holiday in Spain in January, then another in Portugal in February, and various clothes to go with these holidays, you might say, 'Well, yes, I do love you, but is this not a bit extravagant?' But if your daughter had terminal cancer and you knew she would likely be dead in a year, you might ask if she had a last wish. If she said, 'Yes, I would like a world cruise, and the doctor said it would be okay,' would you still say, 'That's too extravagant'? If it were your last opportunity to show your love to your daughter, you would give every penny you could lay your hands on.

If the apostles had understood that Jesus was about to die, and this was the last opportunity they would have to show their gratitude, love and respect for him, how could any of them have found it in their heart to criticize him?

His second justification of her action was, 'so that she may keep it for the day of my burial'. This was going to be the burial that would wipe out death forever.

Suppose you had one million pounds, and you also had a fatal disease. Imagine then that someone came along and said, 'I guarantee that I can cure you. It is expensive medicine, and I will have to charge you nine hundred thousand pounds for it, but if you don't take it you will be dead in six months.' Would you say, 'I can't afford that'? Surely you would say, 'What's money to me if I'm dead? If you can cure me and it takes nine hundred thousand pounds, I'll give you a cheque right now. What's money compared with life?'

If those apostles had woken up to the fact that Jesus was dying to deliver them forever from death, there wouldn't be anything too big for them to give him. Mary had begun to understand what that burial would mean for Christ, and what it would do.

You might say, 'She didn't actually use it for his burial—she wasn't there.' Of course she wasn't; instead of giving it to the poor she now gave it to Christ while he was still alive. He wouldn't need it when he was buried.

The custom of using perfume to anoint the body of departed loved ones was done for practical purposes, to overcome the stench. Corruption did its ugly work when Lazarus was put into the tomb. Martha was right when she said that after four days in the tomb, Lazarus' body would have begun to stink. But when Jesus was laid in the tomb he would see no corruption. That would be the end of the whole process of death; he would rise again! As David said in the Psalms, 'you will not ... let your holy one see corruption' (16:10). He would not need ointment to mask the stench of his death. Mary, along with Martha, had perceived it, and instead of waiting until he died Mary used her money, while she had the chance, in order to show the living Lord how much she valued him.

In the face of all her detractors and critics Christ issued a comment, 'Leave her alone.' John had used the same Greek verb in the story of Lazarus. When Lazarus came out of the tomb, bound with his grave clothes, Christ said, 'Unbind him, and let him go' (John 11:44). No longer was he to be bound by death, nor the fear of it. Now he says of Mary, 'Leave her alone' (12:7). 'Take your hands off; let her be free. Instead of giving it to the poor she has kept it against the day of my burial.'

Here is the command that tells us to get our values in life the right way round and in due proportion. We have a duty to the poor, and no amount of hymn singing will compensate for it if we neglect our duty to them; but let us get our values right. Do you really believe that Jesus died for you in order to break the power of death, to bring you out of the very grave, and to give you a glorious eternal life? If you do, what would you not give him, and what value would you put on him? Would anything be too extravagant?

Let me give you some advice at this moment. Don't wait too long, for when we ourselves are dead we can't give him anything. My advice would be, do it now while life gives the opportunity, so that we may get our proportions right. Mary anointed our Lord Jesus with ointment in preparation for his burial because, along with her sister Martha, she had discovered him to be the Christ, the Son of God who was to come into the world; the resurrection and the life. She didn't wait until he had died and was buried before she anointed him, but spent her vast sum on him beforehand.

From Washing All Over *to* Washing Feet

THE WORK CHRIST DOES TO CLEANSE US

Now before the Feast of the Passover, when Jesus knew that his hour had come to depart out of this world to the Father, having loved his own who were in the world, he loved them to the end.

During supper, when the devil had already put it into the heart of Judas Iscariot, Simon's son, to betray him, Jesus, knowing that the Father had given all things into his hands, and that he had come from God and was going back to God, rose from supper. He laid aside his outer garments, and taking a towel, tied it round his waist. Then he poured water into a basin and began to wash the disciples' feet and to wipe them with the towel that was wrapped around him.

He came to Simon Peter, who said to him, 'Lord, do you wash my feet?'

Jesus answered him, 'What I am doing you do not understand now, but afterwards you will understand.'

Peter said to him, 'You shall never wash my feet.'

Jesus answered him, 'If I do not wash you, you have no share with me.'

Simon Peter said to him, 'Lord, not my feet only but also my hands and my head!'

Jesus said to him, 'The one who has bathed does not need to wash, except for his feet, but is completely clean. And you are clean, but not every one of you.' For he knew who was to betray him; that was why he said, 'Not all of you are clean.'

John 13:1–11

A time to learn

Chapters 13–16 of John's Gospel lead us through what can be called Christ's school of holiness. While some of the later lessons were taught along the way to Gethsemane, Christ taught the early lessons, appropriately enough, in the quiet seclusion of a private guest room where he and his apostles had met to celebrate the Jewish Passover. As they reclined in oriental fashion around the meal table in intimate, heart-to-heart fellowship, Christ showed them that holiness is not primarily a question of keeping rules and regulations (though there are plenty of commandments to keep) but a question of our response of love to the love of God shown to us through his Son, Jesus Christ.

It is at the beginning of these lessons that John records for us an act by our Lord Jesus that no one else has anywhere recorded, namely that in the middle of the Last Supper, he rose from the table, set aside his outer clothes, girded himself with a towel, poured water into a basin and began to wash his disciples' feet. As we read it we get the idea that this particular act was going to set the scene for all the conversation that subsequently followed. Let us think of this act in its own particular context, and listen to hear what it has to say to us; each of us with our own particular need for the cleansing that the Lord Jesus offers if we will come to him.

Washing his disciples' feet

John tells us that the Lord Jesus, in the course of the supper, took a bowl of water and began to wash his disciples' feet. It comes to be, therefore, in the very first place, a tremendous lesson in humility. He himself so applies it, for the Gospel tells us:

> When he had washed their feet and put on his outer garments and resumed his place, he said to them, 'Do you understand what I have done to you? You call me Teacher and Lord, and you are right, for so I am. If I then, your Lord and Teacher, have washed your feet, you also ought to wash one another's feet. For I have given you an example, that you also should do just as I have done to you.' (John 13:12–15)

This is the first lesson then. It is a practical lesson in the Christian duty of humble service to others, and the early church took the lesson very seriously. For instance, the Apostle Paul, talking to Timothy about the question of enrolling widows and supporting them from church funds, says, 'Yes, but you must first enquire as to how this woman has behaved. Has she lived a lazy life, or has she truly served other people? Has she "washed the feet of the saints"?'—meaning, has she humbly and selflessly given herself to the service of others? (See 1 Tim 5:9–10.)

But it is evident as well that this washing of the disciples' feet conveyed not only a practical lesson in humility but, at a deeper level, a profound lesson in spiritual cleansing. That became clear when the Lord Jesus came to Peter, and Peter began to object.

I admire him for doing it. I nurse in my heart a secret wish that Peter was the first man the Lord came to; because, if those other gentlemen, John and James, had sat there and let the Lord wash their feet without any protest, then I should not think so highly of them. Therefore, Peter was, we hope, the first one he came to.

Peter protested at once, 'Lord, you're never going to wash my feet!' In those days, washing somebody's feet was the job you gave to a lowly servant or even a slave. That the Lord should rise and bow at his disciples' feet and wash them was a staggering thing, and Peter protested. But the Lord cut him off, corrected him and said, 'What I am doing you do not understand now, but afterwards you will understand' (John 13:7).

'Oh,' Peter said to him, 'you will never wash my feet.'

But the Lord said, 'Look, Peter, if I don't wash you, you don't have any part with me.'

Peter, going as usual from one extreme to another, and being there to put the Lord right when he felt the Lord needed to be put right, said, 'Well, if that's so, then not only my feet but also my hands and my head!'

And Jesus replied, 'The one who has bathed does not need to wash, except for his feet, but is completely clean. And you are clean, but not every one of you' (13:10). So obviously the Lord has now moved far beyond saying that this is a simple lesson in humility; it is a deeper, profoundly spiritual, lesson.

Two levels of washing

We begin learning what that spiritual lesson is by noticing that there are two levels with this cleansing by water. There is what Jesus calls being 'bathed' all over, and then there is what he calls a 'washing' of the feet. He asserts that if a man has once been bathed, he only needs to rinse his feet, but the rest of him is otherwise clean.

He is, of course, borrowing from the day-to-day experience of people in the east in those far-off days. Very few people had private bathrooms and all of the modern conveniences. If you wanted a bath, you had to go down to the public baths where, of course, you bathed all over. Being bathed all over, you had to walk home, and by the time you got home your feet would have been dusty and dirty with the dust of the road, and the grit between your toes decidedly uncomfortable. But when you got home, you didn't bathe all over again; what you had to do was simply to rinse your feet. And the Lord Jesus was saying that there is in the spiritual realm something that answers to that. There is an initial bathing all over, once and for all, that never needs to be repeated; but then there is a necessity for the constant rinsing of hands and feet.

The bathing all over
Some people have thought that by the bathing all over Christ was referring to the fact that he can cleanse our consciences from the guilt of our sins, because when he died on the cross and poured out his blood, he paid the penalty of our sins. Now, of course, it is wonderfully true that the moment we put our trust in Christ, God assures us that the blood of Jesus Christ, his Son, cleanses us from all sin (1 John 1:7); and so thorough and complete is that cleansing that God can promise us: 'I will remember their sins and their lawless deeds no more' (Heb 10:17). But when our Lord wanted to symbolize the fact that through his blood we have the cleansing and forgiveness of our sins, he filled a cup with wine (not water), gave it to his disciples and told them to drink it—not bathe themselves in it (Matt 26:27–28). The symbol that he used in the enacted parable in John 13, however, was not wine, representing his blood, but water. It points, then, to that other magnificent, once for all, cleansing which Christ offers to all who come to him in true repentance and faith: the washing of regeneration.

What then is the bathing all over? The 'bathing all over' is that once-and-for-all experience of regeneration that occurs when a believer first trusts the Saviour and receives the Holy Spirit. It is called a 'washing' because what the Holy Spirit does is to take his inspired word and apply it to the heart of the sinner, inducing repentance: getting the man or woman to change his or her mind to agree with what God says, to accept God's standards instead of their own inadequate moral standards, and to agree with God that they have fallen short and are powerless to attain to those standards. This is the way the Holy Spirit begins to cleanse a person, by applying the word of God to induce repentance.

But then, of course, there is the positive side to it. There is the regeneration, there is the new life, when the Holy Spirit speaks the word of God creatively into the person's heart. Just as at creation he worked to bring out of the dark, formless, shapeless chaos a living world, so does the Holy Spirit speak in the believer's heart to produce new spiritual life.

That experience happens when we first become Christians, and it needs never to be repeated. Babies, once born, cannot and need not be physically born again; but, having been once born, they can become dirty and have constantly to be cleansed. Even so, when we have received Christ and we have received new spiritual life, and become children of God, we don't have to be born spiritually again, once more or constantly; but we do need constantly to allow the Lord, so to speak, to rinse our feet, because this world is a dirty place.

Christians, as they walk through this world, will find that some of the dirt and filth of this world begins to brush off on them. And in addition they will find that it provokes their own inner maladjustments: they will become angry or envious or fretful, and these attitudes will spoil and defile their spirits. They will need constantly to come to the Lord and to his word to allow that word to wash away those impurities.

So, then, we have two things: we have the initial washing that is once for all, and we have the constant cleansing of the feet.

Learning the lessons

Now, if those are the major lessons of the passage, let's try to put them into their detailed context. It is obvious that the Lord Jesus was about to teach his disciples a fundamental lesson in holiness. This is the very first lesson that we shall all have to learn if we are to be holy—that we need this basic cleansing of being born again; and then that we need this constant rinsing, that is, the 'washing of water by the word' (see Eph 5:25–27). How would he teach the lesson?

Simply, but dramatically, John begins to describe the scene. Here are the disciples sitting or reclining on the cushions by the table. Jesus is going to leave them presently; he's going to die; he's going back to heaven. They are going to be left in a hostile and filthy world. He must teach them these lessons of holiness. As he looks at them, he knows everything, of course. John tells us that he knew his hour had come; he knew that Judas was going to betray him; and he knew that Peter was going to deny him. He could see John and James with their excitable temperaments—men who would willingly cry down the wrath and fire and brimstone of heaven on anybody who got in their way (see Luke 9:51–56). They were a very mixed group, and he knew them perfectly. How would he begin to cleanse their characters and make their personalities sweeter and fresher?

It's a difficult thing, isn't it, to touch somebody's personality? I can tell you it would be, if you tried it sometime with me! Come up to me and say, 'You are insufferably proud, and a hopeless old spoilsport.' Well, you would probably be speaking the truth, but I wouldn't necessarily throw my arms around your neck and say, 'Oh, what a wonderful person you are for telling me. I do enjoy being told that!' In fact, if you're not careful, you are liable to have the very opposite effect from what you intend. You'll make me close up, and I shall become all defensive and argue that I'm better than you, and better than most people anyway.

Our Lord knows better than to adopt that approach. He is going to talk to these men about their personality difficulties, their behavioural difficulties, and he wants them to have such confidence that they are prepared to open their hearts and let him put his finger on the sore spot. So he gets up and quietly girds himself with a towel and begins to wash their feet.

If I could go home tonight, ring a bell and along came a servant who took my shoes off, brought my slippers and got the bath ready for me, I would think I was somebody special. What would you think if you could go home, ring a bell, and the Son of God appeared with a basin, took your shoes off and began to wash your feet?

It is staggering, isn't it? Peter found it embarrassing. We may be sure it wasn't mere ostentation on Christ's part. He got down at their feet to do that menial task because he genuinely loved them. They were the important men—he the servant. Because in his estimation they were important, he served them and cleansed them. He did it because he loved them, not because he enjoyed criticizing them. How gently he washed their feet! And when he wiped them, the towel was warm with the warmth of his own body. What a wonderful Saviour this is, who, even in the moment that he must point out the dirt and the blemishes and the spots and the wrinkles, makes us feel the warmth of his personal love and personal devotion.

The effectiveness of the cleansing

Here we shall need to maintain a proper and healthy balance. There are times in our spiritual lives, even as Christians, when we feel that we have blotted our characters and that all is hopeless. At that time we shall have to remember our Lord's wonderful, triumphant word: 'The one who has bathed does not need to wash, except for his feet, but is completely clean.' The cleansing that Christ provides starts with this cleansing of regeneration, this being born again, and once that has happened it never needs to be repeated. It is a cleansing that in itself is utterly perfect.

We do well to remember this in days when Satan would cause us to doubt. He will say, 'There you are; you say you are a Christian. Just listen to yourself and that conversation you had just now. You really lost your temper, didn't you? And you were bitter. Can you call yourself a Christian after that?' But in those moments of despair, we should remember our Lord's words, and say to ourselves, 'If I have really trusted Christ, if I have been born again, then I have been bathed all over, and it never needs to be repeated.'

And tell me, between a 'being bathed all over' and a 'rinsing of the feet', which would you say is the more important? Which is the bigger thing? Would you not say it is being bathed all over? Of course it is; and the person who has trusted Christ knows that the biggest thing that pertains to their sanctification has already happened, and it never needs to be repeated.

But lest we should grow careless, and say, 'Well, because I trusted Christ five years ago and I was born again, now it doesn't really matter how I live', we should remember our Lord's words, 'you must let me rinse your feet, because if you don't let me rinse your feet, you can have no part with me.' What did he mean by that?

No share with Christ

If we are to answer this question satisfactorily, we shall need to notice, in the first place, exactly what our Lord said. Some translations have not thought it necessary to report his words exactly, and they say: 'If I wash you not, you have no part *in* me', which is a most unfortunate mistake, for our Lord did not say that. He said, 'You have no part *with* me', and that is very different. Once a person is born again and receives God's Holy Spirit, he or she is baptized into the body of Christ and there is thereafter no severance. They are in Christ, and in Christ for ever.

Our Lord was not talking, then, about the question of being *in* him, but of having practical fellowship, having part *with* him in his work and ministry. He was saying to Peter, and to us all, that if we would have practical day-to-day fellowship with him in his work of blessing others, we shall need to submit to his constant washing of our feet.

As believers we are not sinless. Even though we have been born again, have received God's Holy Spirit and are children of God, with his assurance that we shall never perish, the New Testament would have us notice that we still have sin in us. It is still grievously possible for us to 'live according to the flesh', as Paul puts it (Rom 8:12).

Suppose my next door neighbour's boy gets a new bicycle and insists on cycling through my front gates into my garden and knocking down all my tulips. I may be within my rights to explode and scream and shout at him or his mother, or both. But I shall need to watch myself, for if I allow my temper to get out of hand, it will be pretty difficult for me the next day to turn round and tell her how much Jesus loves sinners, and how patient he is. She will rightly say that if I am any example of what Christ does for people, she would prefer he would not do it.

If we want to have practical fellowship with Christ and his work, we must let him constantly 'wash our feet', and cleanse away these defiling eruptions.

More than that. There have been situations when a person has been terribly wronged, and we have said to ourselves, 'If I was in his place I would do this or that.' Yet the person goes and does the very opposite thing. He has mercy; he is kind and patient. We cannot understand him. Why? Because our outlook is different, and as long as we do not understand him there will be a gap between us.

Our experience of Christ is like that. We may belong to him, be children of God born again by his Holy Spirit, but unless we allow him to clear away our unworthy attitudes, there will be a gap between all our attitudes and reactions and his. We shall not be able to take in totally what it is to go out and seek the lost, and to have compassion on the fallen. We shall think it is enough to remain prim and proper in our very respectable drawing rooms. If we are to have this practical fellowship with Christ, we need this constant rinsing of our feet.

The need for constant cleansing

To sum up what we are thinking about, we can do no better than to learn from the writings of Peter. As we shall consider in a later chapter, one of the lovable things about Peter is that although he often made appalling mistakes, yet in the end he did learn his lessons and therefore makes a very kindly teacher.

When our Lord went to wash Peter's feet, he tried to stop him. Then he went to the other extreme and wanted him to bathe his hands and his head as well, and our Lord had to tell him that that was not necessary. But he *had* learned the vital lesson about this initial cleansing.

In Acts 15, Luke tells us that at one stage in the early Church's history, a very great meeting was held when the apostles decided to send out a letter to tell the world at large how a person is saved, and in particular how a Gentile is to be saved. There were those in the Jewish community who thought that the way to get Gentile Christians living holy lives was to impose all sorts of rules and regulations upon them, such as circumcision.

Peter stood up in that council and said: 'No! Even we ourselves, true blooded Jews, have to be saved simply by the grace of God; and now we have before us evidence in the conversion of Cornelius and his colleagues, that God gives the Holy Spirit to the Gentiles when they believe; making no difference between them and us, he has "cleansed their hearts by faith"' (see 15:6–11).

In the context, the contrast is between trying to cleanse yourself by external ordinances, and being cleansed by personal faith in the

Lord Jesus. Peter is referring to what happened at the conversion of these Gentiles: when they first received the Holy Spirit, they were cleansed by faith.

Again in 1 Peter 1:22, talking to Christians, he says the same thing: 'Having purified your souls by your obedience to the truth …'. This basic purification is when a person faces the word of God and learns that he or she is unsaved and unholy and needs to be born again, and submits to that truth. So that person's soul is purified by their obedience to the truth: 'since you have been born again, not of perishable seed but of imperishable, through the living and abiding word of God' (1:23). So Peter had learned the first, basic lesson.

Then he learned the next lesson: the need for constant rinsing of the feet. To these people who had been born again, who had purified their souls by faith, he says in this same letter, 'Put away all malice and all deceit and hypocrisy and envy and all slander.' He is telling them that, since they are like newborn infants, they must put those things away, and instead 'long for the pure spiritual milk, that by it you may grow up into salvation' (2:1–2). There is always the need for this constant putting away, this rinsing of the feet.

A final question

Let's read again what John tells us was on Christ's mind, just before he rose to serve them.

> When Jesus knew that his hour had come to depart out of this world to the Father, having loved his own who were in the world, he loved them to the end. During supper, when the devil had already put it into the heart of Judas Iscariot, Simon's son, to betray him, Jesus, knowing that the Father had given all things into his hands, and that he had come from God and was going back to God, rose from supper. He laid aside his outer garments, and taking a towel, tied it round his waist. (John 13:1–4)

He saw them all sitting there, and he knew their difficulties. He knew, for instance, how deep the wounds in Peter's personality went, and yet it was not in any spirit of defeat that he rose from the table. He knew what Satan was planning to do to that little company to blast them open, to prey on Peter's weakness and to get Peter to deny him and blot his spiritual copybook almost beyond recovery.

Yet the Lord Jesus rose from supper to begin the work anyway, because he knew that he had come from God and was going to God, and that the Father had put all things into Christ's hand and that he himself was equal to the task of cleansing his people. And it is with such a Saviour firmly before our minds that we may ask ourselves, indeed we should ask him, what level of cleansing we require, and then let him do what he has promised he will do.

From the Light *into* Darkness

JUDAS REJECTS THE
FRIENDSHIP OF JESUS

After saying these things, Jesus was troubled in his spirit, and testified, 'Truly, truly, I say to you, one of you will betray me.'

The disciples looked at one another, uncertain of whom he spoke. One of his disciples, whom Jesus loved, was reclining at table close to Jesus, so Simon Peter motioned to him to ask Jesus of whom he was speaking.

So that disciple, leaning back against Jesus, said to him, 'Lord, who is it?'

Jesus answered, 'It is he to whom I will give this morsel of bread when I have dipped it.' So when he had dipped the morsel, he gave it to Judas, the son of Simon Iscariot. Then after he had taken the morsel, Satan entered into him.

Jesus said to him, 'What you are going to do, do quickly.' Now no one at the table knew why he said this to him. Some thought that, because Judas had the money bag, Jesus was telling him, 'Buy what we need for the feast,' or that he should give something to the poor. So, after receiving the morsel of bread, he immediately went out. And it was night.

John 13:21–30

A hard lesson

The original setting of the course of lessons in the Upper Room was poignant indeed. For three years Christ had lived, worked and travelled with the twelve men who were his apostles; and they all (except one) had loved him, served him, and sacrificed home comforts and worldly wealth in order to follow him. It is that one exception whom we will now consider.

The opposite of holiness

The first major lesson in Christ's school of holiness began with the powerfully symbolic object lesson of Christ washing his disciples' feet. The second major lesson consists of another momentous symbolic gesture: Christ giving the morsel of bread to Judas. The giving of that bread did two things: first, it unmistakably identified the traitor; and secondly, it vividly exposed the nature of his sin.

John's first reason for recording this event is, doubtless, that it actually happened. But the event is more than history: it carries a universal lesson that we need to learn. Its relevance is this: our Lord's washing of his disciples' feet teaches us that true believers are expected to 'cleanse [themselves] from every defilement of body and spirit, bringing holiness to completion in the fear of God' (2 Cor 7:1). Granted, then, that we should aim at becoming ever more holy, how shall we do that unless we have a clear idea of what holiness is? And not merely what particular attitudes and acts are holy, but what the essence and heart of holiness is.

Now, one way of learning what a thing is, is to be shown its opposite. We learn, for instance, to appreciate beauty all the more by being shown ugliness. We become acutely aware of what it means to be healthy, when we lose our health and become sick. What, then is the opposite of holiness?

'Sin, of course!' says someone; and that is correct as far as it goes. But sin expresses itself in many ways. As the opposite of *righteousness*, for instance, sin is lawlessness, says the Bible (1 John 3:4). It is living in total disregard of God's law, as if God's law did not exist. But what is sin as the opposite of *holiness*?

It is this that the Lord Jesus is about to teach us. In identifying the traitor, Judas, and in vividly exposing the nature of his sin, he will show us what the very essence of unholiness is. We shall then perceive all the more clearly what its opposite, true holiness, is and what the secret is of attaining holiness.

The essence of unholiness

We have already heard Christ describing Judas's sin (without naming him) in the words, 'He who ate my bread has lifted his heel against me' (John 13:18). Now our Lord adds the even darker phrase: 'One of you will betray me' (v. 21). We know from the other Gospels that Judas betrayed the Lord for money: he sold him for thirty pieces of silver (see Matt 26:15). We must put all these elements together to get a comprehensive view of Judas's sin.

Let's go back, then, to the phrase, 'He who ate *my bread*'. It was not a question of thirteen men sharing a meal together in a restaurant, with each man paying his own share of the cost of the meal. On this occasion, as on many occasions in the past, Jesus was the host who, in his loving generosity, had invited Judas as his personal guest to come and share his table. In addition to the food on his table, the Lord Jesus had bestowed on Judas several high privileges and gifts. He had appointed him as an apostle, and commissioned him to go out as his envoy along with the other apostles to preach the gospel of the kingdom of God. It may even be that Judas was empowered like the other apostles to do miracles, for, though Judas was never anything else than an unbeliever (and our Lord knew that, according to John 6:70–71), it is possible for people who are not believers to do miracles in the name of Jesus (see Matt 7:22–23). In addition, Judas was trusted with the position of treasurer of the apostolic group: he held the purse which contained all the money that Jesus owned (from which purse, incidentally, Judas often misappropriated the funds, John 12:6).

But far beyond these high privileges, gifts and honoured duties, Christ had offered Judas his personal friendship. Christ could have treated Judas as a non-commissioned officer in an army who, important though his rank might be, would never be invited to dine with the supreme commander of the army, let alone with the president of the country. But no! Jesus had habitually invited Judas to his table, offering him not only his food but his personal friendship.

And Judas's sin? He had taken all Christ's gifts, accepted all the privileges, eaten the very food off Christ's table—and had no time, love or loyalty for Christ personally. Yes, he had pretended to be Christ's friend and loyal servant. But he had never loved Christ. And as for loyalty, when the opportunity came, he would not only steal Christ's money from the bag; he would sell Christ's friendship, and Christ himself into the bargain.

The seriousness of Judas's sin

Now there are some things in life so sacred that one could not put a monetary value on them, and anyone who was prepared to sell these things for money would be heartily despised by all right thinking people. Friendship is one of these. Loyalty is another. A man who spies on a foreign country may well be admired by his fellow-citizens for his courage and skill. But a man who is prepared to sell his own country, so long as the price is high enough, is regarded by his fellow-countrymen with loathing and disgust, as guilty of the most appalling perversion of true values. If detected and caught he will normally be imprisoned for life or even executed. And what would we say of a man who would sell his mother into slavery for a handsome fee?

So for Judas to take all Christ's gifts and then to steal his money from the common purse was certainly a mean and despicable trick. But in the end, what would the loss of a few coins mean to Christ? For Judas to take all Christ's gifts, to sit as his guest, pretend friendship, eat the very food off his table, and then sell both Christ himself and his friendship for money—that was to strike a dagger personally into Christ's very heart. Christ was no unfeeling stoic. Years later, as John recalled the scene and recorded it for us, he still could picture in his mind the distress Jesus showed as he made the announcement: '[he] was troubled in his spirit, and testified, "Truly, truly, I say to you, one of you will betray me"' (13:21).

But more, if Jesus had been simply an ordinary man, or even a uniquely brilliant theologian and teacher, Judas's treachery would still have been infamous. Jesus was no ordinary man; he was the Son of God. To take Jesus' gifts and food, and then reject him, was the same as taking God's gifts and then rejecting God. To sell Jesus and his friendship was to sell God and his friendship. The dagger Judas thrust into the heart of Jesus penetrated the very heart of God.

Judas's heart: a microcosm of humankind

Judas's behaviour may seem to us extreme; but his attitude of heart is more common than you might think. Judas took Christ's gifts, but he had no time, love or loyalty for Christ personally. And multitudes take and enjoy God's gifts, but have no time, love or loyalty for God either. They treat God the creator as Judas treated Christ. All around us spread out for our enjoyment are the good and often delightful gifts of nature, our daily bread included. But there is more to life than the impersonal forces of nature. Behind nature there beats the throbbing heart of a personal creator; and nature's gifts are his loving invitations to us to seek him and his personal friendship. Multitudes take and enjoy the gifts but have no interest in the divine giver. They own no debt of gratitude to him, no love for him, no loyalty to him, no desire for his friendship. They ignore him. Worse still, to get more money, better positions in society, more acceptance with the world, many are prepared to sell God's Son and to barter faith in God for worldly success. This is the very heart and essence of unholiness. To be unholy you don't have to murder anyone, raid a bank, commit adultery, or torture little children. All you have to do is to take God's gifts and have no love or time for God himself. By that process you wound the very heart of God and desacralize everything in life as well.

An ancient sin

This false, unholy attitude of heart is the sin into which Satan originally lured Adam and Eve. Genesis 3 describes how he pointed to the tree of the knowledge of good and evil and made Eve aware that it was good for food, that is, for physical satisfaction; that it was good to look at, that is, for aesthetic satisfaction; and desirable to make one wise, that is, intellectual satisfaction. Then he put to Eve the lie that it is possible to enjoy these lovely things—in a word, to enjoy life to the full independently of God and without regard either for him or for his word. Adam and Eve believed the lie and inevitably it reorientated humankind's attitude to life, to its resources and relationships. Life's benefits ceased to be regarded as gifts from the gracious hand of God to be enjoyed in fellowship with God, drawing their hearts into ever closer friendship with him, so that, when life on earth ceased and life's temporary gifts were gone, the friendship would continue eternally in God's heaven. Now life's benefits became an end in themselves, drawing their hearts away from God instead of to him. Moreover, their alienation from God made them afraid of him. He was someone to hide from, no longer a source of their enjoyment of life but a threat to it. And the poison of this false attitude to God has infiltrated the veins of every human being.

It is the world's typical sin; so much so that the Bible often uses the word 'world' in a bad sense to refer to human society, organized and living on the basis of this false heart-attitude to God. We find many examples of this later on in Christ's course on holiness.

Moreover, unregenerate people are not the only ones to be marked by this sin. Genuine believers are still drawn to it, and need to be exhorted in the words of the Apostle John, 'Do not love the world or the things in the world. If anyone loves the world, the love of the Father is not in him. For all that is in the world—the desires of the flesh and the desires of the eyes and pride of life—is not from the Father but is from the world' (see 1 John 2:15–16). It is not that the beautiful things in life, or even the desire for them, are wrong in themselves. The Bible says that God has given us all things richly to enjoy (1 Tim 6:17). The damage is done when the lovely things of life (or anything else, for that matter) are allowed to steal our hearts away from God. That is worldliness and the very essence of unholiness.

Let's suppose a wealthy man decided to mark his son's eighteenth birthday by giving him a private aeroplane. And suppose the son took the gift without thanking his father, climbed into the cockpit, flew off and never returned to visit his father again throughout the rest of his life. What would we think of the son? And how would the father feel?

The essence of holiness

If this, then, is the basic principle of unholiness, we may at once deduce that the essential nature of holiness is its exact opposite. It is not so much the keeping of a list of rules, although Christ later on reminds us that if we love him, we shall keep his commandments. At heart, true holiness is unswerving love and devotion to the divine persons.

Failure to grasp this has sometimes led people to the observance of all kinds of legalistic practices which have an outward show of holiness, but lack its basic principle. There are some Christians, for instance, who still wear mediaeval clothes, in the belief that to wear modern dress would be unholy. It is not for us, of course, to judge the inner state of their hearts; but we can be sure of this, that it is possible to wear antiquated clothes and to keep all kinds of rigid codes of conduct, and yet at heart have little or no love for the Saviour, or active devotion to him personally. Even preachers and theologians are not immune to this danger. It is possible to study holy Scripture as a mere profession or hobby, and to preach the Bible for the sheer joy of the sense of power it gives the preacher over large congregations, and yet at heart to be distant from the Lord, and lacking in personal love for him. And it is also possible for preachers—let Judas warn us—for the sake of position, career or gain, to be disloyal to Christ morally, spiritually and theologically.

If we are going to be progressively more holy, we must become ever more devoted to the Lord, love him more dearly and serve him more loyally. But if that is so, the most fervent believers will be the first to admit that their love for Christ is not as warm and constant as it should be. The pressures of life, its joys, sorrows and struggles, exhaust the heart's energies, distract its loyalties and cool its affections towards Christ. What can unfreeze them and renew their devotion? And how will Christ, who sees and knows the fickleness of our hearts and their disloyalties to him, react towards us? Will he denounce and reject us?

That very question drives us back to the Upper Room to watch Christ's reaction to Judas and to observe how he identified the traitor and by what means he exposed his treachery.

The exposure of humanity's treachery

By the time that the Lord Jesus announced, 'One of you will betray me', Judas must finally have realized that Jesus knew what he was scheming to do. But as yet none of the others in the Upper Room knew who the traitor was; and they stared at one another at a loss to know which of them Jesus was referring to. One of them, the apostle whom Jesus loved, was reclining next to Jesus. Peter therefore motioned to this disciple to get him to ask Jesus which one of them he meant. So, leaning back against Jesus, this disciple asked him directly, 'Lord, who is it?'

Now came the dramatic moment when Jesus must expose the traitor. How would he do it? He could have done it by silently pointing an accusing finger at him, while Judas squirmed in his seat. But he did not choose to do it that way. He could have done it by naming Judas in the course of a withering denunciation of his treachery. That would have been terrifying.

Perhaps we can recall some of the other occasions when our Lord was obliged to expose the sin of evil men. How awesome, for instance, must have been the sight of his flashing eyes and uplifted whip, as he drove the money-changers out of the temple (John 2:14–17). How withering must have been his denunciation of certain teachers of the law and certain Pharisees: 'You brood of vipers, how are you to escape being sentenced to hell?' (Matt 23:33). But the sins that moved our Lord on those occasions to such trenchant public rebuke were the desecration of God's house, the misrepresentation of God's character, the persecution of God's prophets, and the oppression of the poor under the guise of religion. Christ would not stand by and see other people being spiritually damaged through the religious perversities of hypocritical men.

But now in the Upper Room it was not other people who were about to be damaged. Judas's sin was hurting Christ personally, thrusting a poisoned arrow at Christ's own heart. How, then, and in what terms, and in what tone of voice, and by what action would he expose this viper's treachery against his own person? In answer to John's question as to who the traitor was, he said, 'It is the one to whom I will give this piece of bread, when I have dipped it in the dish.' Then, dipping the piece of bread, he gave it to Judas Iscariot, the son of Simon.

This eloquent action was more than a convenient way of indicating who the traitor was. Judas, we remember, had for the last three years been taking Christ's bread, pretending to be his friend. Now, by betraying Christ, he was about to fling the bread of Christ's friendship back into his face. How would Christ react to that? By offering him once more that self-same bread! There was no burning indignation, no bitter rebuke. Only the offer of that piece of bread, which said with unspoken eloquence: 'Judas, you have taken the bread of my friendship, and, in spite of it, you have treacherously lifted up your heel to kick me. Now you are about to betray me. I know all about it. But, even so, before you do it, Judas, I offer you once more the bread of my friendship. Will you not accept it?'

The gesture was neither cynical nor sarcastic. Nor was it a bribe to curry favour with Judas. It was a genuine, last minute attempt to save him from his self-chosen hell. According to the unwritten laws of ancient Middle Eastern hospitality, if a host took a piece of bread, dipped it in the dish and personally handed it to one of his guests, it did not only mean that he was honouring the guest by offering him an especially tasteful morsel of food from the banquet: it meant in addition that he was pledging himself to that guest to be his loyal friend. And we may be sure that, even at this dark and dramatic moment in Judas's pathway to hell, our Lord's offering to him of the bread was a genuine gesture, late as the time was, to urge upon Judas his friendship and love and with them the forgiveness, the pardon and the eventual glory that they implied.

Judas's reaction

We are not told how Judas felt at that moment. Poor Judas! Why did he not cry out in the wretchedness of his heart, 'Lord, I didn't know you knew; but now I see that you have found me out. I am consumed with this dastardly, despicable lust for money and for power that drives me to sell and betray you. But if, knowing all about it, you can still offer me the bread of your loyal friendship, then I need it above everything else. The devil himself seems to have got hold of me and is dragging me down to hell. Save me from myself! Save me from my appalling perversion.' We may be sure that if Judas had so cried out, he would have found that Christ's gesture in offering him the bread was genuine indeed. Christ would have saved him and remained loyal to him for ever. As it was, Judas took it; but once more it was a hypocritical action. He took the piece of bread he was given but, utterly unrepentant, he continued with his schemes to betray the giver.

He had made his final decision. 'Then,' says John, 'Satan entered into him ... So, after receiving the morsel of bread, he immediately went out' (John 13:27, 30).

What would Christ's reaction be to this further and final rejection of his friendship and salvation? There came no violent thunderbolt of denunciation. All Christ said was, as Judas passed through the door, 'What you are about to do, do quickly.' At the time no one at the table understood what this meant. They thought, says John, that since Judas had charge of the money, Christ was telling him to buy what was needed for the feast, or to give something to the poor. Just imagine, if you can, in what tone of voice and accompanied by what looks and body gestures Jesus would normally have told his disciples to give something to the poor. It was in that tone of voice that our Lord made his final comment to Judas.

Even so, John's recording of the disciples' misreading of Christ's words to Judas is poignant in the extreme. It recalls the incident that John has recorded a few verses earlier (12:1–8). We recall how on that occasion Mary, the sister of Lazarus, had expressed her gratitude, love and devotion to the Lord Jesus by anointing his feet with a flask full of expensive ointment worth at least a whole year's wages. To Judas such extreme devotion to Christ seemed absurdly excessive, and he voiced his criticism: 'Why was this ointment not sold for three hundred denarii and given to the poor?' John adds that Judas did not really care for the poor. He was a thief; and since he held the common purse, if the ointment had been sold and the proceeds had been temporarily put into the purse, he might well have helped himself to some of it. But away and beyond that, what actually annoyed him was that anybody should think Jesus worthy of such extremely expensive devotion, and should love him enough to spend so much on him. He himself had served Jesus while it suited him, for the position, power and money he got out of it. But love Jesus personally? Why would anyone love Jesus like that? He certainly didn't; and he could not understand why anyone else should.

And now he never would understand. Had he accepted not only the morsel of bread, but what it stood for, he would have gone on to discover with ever increasing wonder what the friendship of Christ means for those who accept it. But having taken the bread, he now barricaded his heart for the last time against Christ's love and friendship. Immediately he went out, 'And', says John, 'it was night' (13:30). It was, of course, literally night-time. But the phrase points beyond mere timetable. At that moment Satan, whose suggestions Judas had earlier welcomed as allies in his struggle to maintain his independence of Jesus (13:2), did not go away and leave Judas to his hoped-for freedom. He entered into Judas, overpowered him and made him his minion (13:27). With that, Judas went out into a night of unrelieved moral and spiritual darkness that will never know a dawn. He is but an extreme example of what the Bible warns us will happen to those who finally reject God and his Son.

'But that's terrible', says someone. 'Are you really saying that God would let people go to hell, or even send them there, just for refusing to believe in and accept Jesus Christ? If so, who could respect or believe in a God like that? Is he not supposed to be a God of love?' But this very objection leads us on to consider what Jesus said next when Judas had gone out.

The display of God's glory

Let's get this straight to start with: neither Jesus' choice of Judas to be an apostle, nor his prediction that Judas would betray him, *made* Judas betray him. Suppose, looking down from a helicopter, you saw two cars approaching each other at high speed round a blind corner, you could predict that they were bound to crash into each other. But your prediction, though true, would not make them crash. The crash would be the drivers' fault. And so it was with Judas. Jesus knew in advance and predicted that he would betray him; but that did not make Judas betray him or excuse him for doing it. Judas did what he did of his own free will, out of the sinfulness of his own heart.

Nor did Satan have any intention of fulfilling the Old Testament prophecies that the Messiah must die, when he infiltrated into Judas's mind the idea of betraying Jesus. He too acted out of the scheming of his own mind. To his fallen and devilish way of thinking, the betrayal of Jesus and his death on a cross could only be a disastrous defeat for Jesus. Death by crucifixion was the most opprobrious punishment known to the ancient world. The shame of it would drown the cause of Jesus in an ocean of disgrace. And so he thought it a masterful stroke of strategy when he suborned one of Jesus' chosen apostles to betray him to that public humiliation.

But how mistaken Satan was! The Son of God had come to our world on purpose to die the death of the cross. Knowing in advance that Judas would betray him to that death, he had deliberately chosen him as an apostle. And when Judas finally left the Upper Room to go out to do his dastardly deed, Christ commanded him, 'What you are going to do, do quickly' (13:27). So, far from the shame of the cross destroying the reputation of Christ, the suffering of the cross would become the greatest exhibition of the glory of God and of the Son of God that the world has ever seen, or that the universe will ever see.

Which is why, when Judas had gone out and Christ's crucifixion was now imminent, Christ declared, 'Now is the Son of Man glorified, and God is glorified in him' (13:31).

Even before Satan polluted a human heart with slanderous misrepresentations of God's character, God had been planning and working towards this moment. In due course God's own Son set foot on our rebel planet. Then came the climax when the Creator incarnate came face to face in the Upper Room with the creature who was about to betray him to a cross. Now the world would see what God was like! Now Christ's reaction to this traitor would reveal exactly what was in God's heart. Deliberately, and in full knowledge of what Judas was about to do, he offered Judas the bread of his friendship.

Magnificent though this gesture was, it formed but the prelude to the even more majestic display of God's glory at Calvary. For just as Christ's giving of the morsel of bread to Judas exposed the traitor and his evil treachery, so God's giving of his Son into the hands of mankind exposed our race's rebel hatred against God. 'This is the heir', they said; 'Let us kill him, so that the inheritance may be ours' (Luke 20:14). But even as they nailed his hands and feet to the cross, God was offering Christ to the world as the bread of his friendship, as the pledge of his forgiveness and eternal love to all who would repent and receive him in sincerity and truth. 'In Christ God was reconciling the world to himself, not counting their trespasses against them' (2 Cor 5:19). For 'God shows his love for us in that while we were still sinners, Christ died for us. . . . For if while we were enemies we were reconciled to God by the death of his Son, much more, now that we are reconciled, shall we be saved by his life' (Rom 5:8, 10). And right down to us in our century comes God's call through Christ's apostles:

> We are ambassadors for Christ, God making his appeal through us. We implore you on behalf of Christ, be reconciled to God. For our sake he made him to be sin who knew no sin, so that in him we might become the righteousness of God. (2 Cor 5:20–21)

If after that, people take all the Creator's natural gifts but reject the bread of his friendship, they will, like Judas, go out into a night of eternal darkness where the light of God's friendship never comes and the awareness of his holiness burns like an unquenchable fire. But they will have only themselves to blame.

So when Judas had gone out, Jesus said, as we have already noticed, 'Now is the Son of Man glorified, and God is glorified in him.' But he added, 'If God is glorified in him, God will also glorify him [the Son] in himself, and glorify him at once' (John 13:32).

Jesus was predicting that his death on the cross would be followed by his resurrection and his elevation by God to the position of supreme power in the universe, and by his appointment as the judge and ruler of all. One day, God will require every knee in heaven, earth and hell to bow, and every tongue to confess that Jesus Christ is Lord—worthy to control and administer the wealth of the universe and to receive the submission and worshipful service of every sentient creature. And when God does so, it will be universally acknowledged that God is no tyrant. His moral right to insist on universal submission and worship will have been established not simply in the name of his almighty power, but in the name of Jesus, who humbled himself to wash his creatures' feet, offered the bread of his friendship even to Judas and died for all mankind on the cross.

This is how the New Testament sums it up:

> Christ Jesus, who, though he was in the form of God, did not count equality with God a thing to be grasped, but made himself nothing, taking the form of a servant, being born in the likeness of men. And being found in human form, he humbled himself by becoming obedient to the point of death, even death on a cross. Therefore God has highly exalted him and bestowed on him the name that is above every name, so that at the name of Jesus every knee should bow, in heaven and on earth and under the earth, and every tongue confess that Jesus Christ is Lord, to the glory of God the Father. (Phil 2:5–11)

From Failure *to* Fruitful Service

Simon Peter said to him, 'Lord, where are you going?'

Jesus answered him, 'Where I am going you cannot follow me now, but you will follow afterwards.'

Peter said to him, 'Lord, why can I not follow you now? I will lay down my life for you.'

Jesus answered, 'Will you lay down your life for me? Truly, truly, I say to you, the cock will not crow till you have denied me three times.'

John 13:36–38

Simon Peter followed Jesus, and so did another disciple. Since that disciple was known to the high priest, he entered with Jesus into the court of the high priest, but Peter stood outside at the door. So the other disciple, who was known to the high priest, went out and spoke to the servant girl who kept watch at the door, and brought Peter in.

The servant girl at the door said to Peter, 'You also are not one of this man's disciples, are you?'

He said, 'I am not.'

Now the servants and officers had made a charcoal fire, because it was cold, and they were standing and warming themselves.

Peter also was with them, standing and warming himself. . . . So they said to him, 'You also are not one of his disciples, are you?'

He denied it and said, 'I am not.'

One of the servants of the high priest, a relative of the man whose ear Peter had cut off, asked, 'Did I not see you in the garden with him?' Peter again denied it, and at once a cock crowed.

John 18:15–18, 25–27

When they had finished breakfast, Jesus said to Simon Peter, 'Simon, son of John, do you love me more than these?'

He said to him, 'Yes, Lord; you know that I love you.'

He said to him, 'Feed my lambs.'

He said to him a second time, 'Simon, son of John, do you love me?'

He said to him, 'Yes, Lord; you know that I love you.'

He said to him, 'Tend my sheep.'

He said to him the third time, 'Simon, son of John, do you love me?'

Peter was grieved because he said to him the third time, 'Do you love me?' and he said to him, 'Lord, you know everything; you know that I love you.'

Jesus said to him, 'Feed my sheep. Truly, truly, I say to you, when you were young, you used to dress yourself and walk wherever you wanted, but when you are old, you will stretch out your hands, and another will dress you and carry you where you do not want to go.' (This he said to show by what kind of death he was to glorify God.) And after saying this he said to him, 'Follow me.'

Peter turned and saw the disciple whom Jesus loved following them, the one who had been reclining at table close to him and had said, 'Lord, who is it that is going to betray you?' When Peter saw him, he said to Jesus, 'Lord, what about this man?'

Jesus said to him, 'If it is my will that he remain until I come, what is that to you? You follow me!'

John 21:15–22

A lesson about self-reliance

The last journey that we will consider reminds us that a journey of faith with Jesus is lifelong. The Saviour does not only save people and then leave them to get on with life as best they can. He carries on his work in all of those he has redeemed until the day when he takes them to himself in that place that he is preparing for them (John 14:2–3). And for each follower of the Lord Jesus Christ there will be many lessons to learn along that road.

One of the many lessons we can learn from the experience of the Apostle Peter is moderately easy to agree with in theory, but much more difficult to face when we discover its truth in practical experience. The lesson is this: however grateful to the Lord we may be for what he has done for us, and however determined we may be to love, obey and follow him, our love and determination are not enough in themselves to keep us following him as we should. Indeed we have hidden weaknesses within us that, were we dependent solely on our own resources, would easily ruin the whole procedure completely.

Of course, all believers will unhesitatingly agree that we are still imperfect and sin from time to time; but almost unconsciously many of us assume that, given adequate determination, care and effort, we can manage by ourselves to overcome or suppress our sins and achieve the desired standard of holiness. It just is not true. Sin has sapped our strength and damaged our moral fibre more than we think; and it can be a bitter experience when repeated failure makes us face this unpleasant and disturbing fact.

The great Apostle Paul openly confesses the feeling of utter wretchedness that came over him when he made this discovery. 'I myself serve the law of God', he says, 'with my mind'; for intellectually he saw clearly that serving God was the only sensible way of living. 'I delight', he also says, 'in the law of God, in my inner being'; for living to please God was to him no cold, merely intellectual activity. He delighted in it: it moved him emotionally. Moreover, he says, 'For I have the desire to do what is right'—his determination to live a holy life was driven by an iron will. But all in vain! All too often practice turned out to be the opposite of intention. 'For I do not do the good I want,' he wails, 'but the evil I do not want is what I keep on doing' (Rom 7:15–25). Intellect, emotion and will, all combined, and put to the task of living a holy, Christ-like life, were found to be seriously inadequate. It was a bitter experience for Paul.

God, however, had known it from the very start; and when Paul discovered his bankruptcy, God pointed him to the provision he himself had made so that even a bankrupt Paul might be able to follow, love and obey the Lord Jesus as he should (see Rom 8). And so it will be with us. Using Peter as his object lesson, Christ will now point out to us our inadequacy; and if only we are prepared to take Christ seriously and believe what he says about us, we shall be ready to learn about, and then lay hold of, his provision which brings holiness realistically within our grasp.

Peter: our object lesson

When the Lord remarked that he was going away, and that where he was going his disciples could not come, Peter considered the matter for a few seconds and decided that our Lord was exaggerating things unnecessarily. 'Lord,' said Peter, 'where exactly are you going?' Our Lord replied, 'Where I am going you cannot follow me now, but you will follow later' (John 13:36).

But Peter was not satisfied, for he felt that the Lord's remarks implied a defect in his courage. 'But, Lord,' he said, 'why can't I follow you now? I will lay down my life for you.' He meant every word, for in the past years there had grown up in Peter's heart a deep and warm devotion to the Lord Jesus, and as far as he knew he was perfectly willing to lay down his life for him, if necessary. Certainly he was no Judas; and perhaps in Peter's way of thinking the exposure of Judas's insincerity and treachery had made him feel all the more certain that he would never treat the Lord in this despicable way, but would follow him, if need be, to prison and to death. As far as he knew, then, his devotion to Christ was not to be doubted. The trouble was that he did not know himself anywhere near well enough. Actually, there was in Peter's personality a hidden weakness; and when, in a few hours' time, by the sinister machinations of the devil himself, circumstances exerted unbearable pressure on that weakness, Peter's devotion was going to collapse completely and he would deny the Lord with oaths and curses. This the Lord now had to tell him and expose to him his weakness, as earlier he had exposed Judas's treachery.

Peter's basic mistake

Of course, we must not confuse Peter's weakness with Judas's treachery. Peter's weakness was the weakness of a man who had been *bathed all over*, had experienced the regeneration of the Holy Spirit, had been made completely clean (13:10–11). Judas's treachery was the treachery, not merely of an unregenerate man, but of a man who was led by, and eventually possessed by, the devil (13:2, 10–11, 18, 27). Peter's weakness would eventually be overcome; Judas' treachery would never be reversed.

On the other hand, Peter's weakness would not be overcome automatically. The only way for any of us as believers to overcome our weaknesses is, first to be made to face them and to admit they are there, and then to repent of them and to seek the Lord's grace and the power of the Holy Spirit to overcome them. Had Peter been willing therefore, to listen to the Lord Jesus and to accept that what he said was true, Peter could have spared himself enormous anguish and sorrow. And we might wonder, if we did not know the obtuseness of our own hearts, why Peter did not reply to the Lord Jesus in the following fashion: 'Lord, I cannot believe it. I am not that kind of man. I don't think that I have this weakness that you talk of; but if I have—and you know best—then please tell me now how I may overcome it, and be saved from this ugly thing that you say I am going to do.' If he had said that, the Lord Jesus would most certainly have shown him how he could have avoided the oncoming fall.

But no, Peter could not believe it about himself, not even when the Lord told him. He thought he had resources enough of courage and determination to make any sacrifice that was necessary in the course of his devotion to the Lord. The fact was, he had not. Therefore, he had to learn the hard and bitter way that the Lord knew him and his personality better than he did himself. The weakness that the Lord said he saw in him was really there, and must be brought to the surface before it could be healed. If, then, the only way to make Peter face his weakness, and thus to learn to overcome it, was to allow him to come into circumstances where he would fail, and deny the Lord, then the Lord's love was such that he would allow Peter to come into those circumstances and make that appalling discovery. For, as 13:1 reminds us, 'Having loved his own who were in the world, he loved them to the end'; and his love was determined to make Peter eventually perfectly holy, whatever the cost and the price should be.

The certainty of Peter's restoration

But Christ was certain, of course, that Peter would eventually be restored and triumph. 'Where I am going you cannot follow me now,' he said to Peter, 'but you shall follow afterwards.' And so Peter did. Though his courage left him, and he denied and deserted Christ in order to escape suffering in the high priest's court and at the cross, he was afterwards restored, then served and followed Christ magnificently for many years. Finally, suffering a death like the Lord's, he went home to glory.

And we should not fail to notice this important matter: when the breakdown came, as our Lord predicted, and Peter failed to follow the Lord in his suffering as he should have done, it must have been a tremendous source of encouragement and new hope for Peter to remember what the Lord said before it all happened: 'You cannot follow me now, *but you will follow afterwards*.' All through the ups and downs of the rest of Peter's life, he would constantly have repeated the Lord's words to himself over and over again, giving them their fullest meaning. He had not yet been allowed to follow the ascended Lord bodily into the glory of the Father's presence in heaven. But there was no doubt that he would one day. Christ had said he would; and his promise would not fail. And what is more, entry into the glory of the Father's presence in heaven, and the direct sight of the blessed Lord Jesus, would instantaneously complete Peter's sanctification and complete it forever beyond danger of any further collapse. This too, then, our Lord let Peter know by implication, before he fell. The certainty of this promise and the courage it gave him enabled him to face his failure, to come back, and follow the Lord devotedly for the rest of his life. And since Christ has no favourites, all who trust him may take this same promise to themselves.

Peter's restoration

Let's come now to those other lessons that stand at the end of John's Gospel, lessons that would help prepare Peter for a life of service and finally for his own death. The risen Christ and his disciples had just finished their breakfast on the beach. Now Peter was to be reappointed. First of all he had been a fisher of men (Matt 4:19), now he is going to be appointed as a shepherd of the sheep.

Listen to how the Lord searched the man's heart. Calling him by his original name, he said, 'Simon, son of John, do you love me?'

'Yes, Lord,' he said, 'you know that I love you.'

He said to him, 'Tend my lambs.' Then a second time he said to him, 'Simon, son of John, do you love me?'

He said to him, 'Yes, Lord; you know that I love you.'

Jesus said to him, 'Tend my sheep.'

When he asked him for the third time, Peter said, 'Lord, you know everything; you know that I love you. Didn't you know before? I didn't know my own heart but you knew, Lord. You told me that I would deny you. I didn't think it was possible, but you knew. You know everything, and you know, Lord, that I love you.'

And this was not boasting, for where would Peter have been without the Lord? This was not the pride of an eminently successful and spiritual man; it was the humble tribute of a sheep, who would have perished forever apart from Christ's work as a shepherd.

'I love you Lord', he said. 'I would have been lost without you.'

'Then, Peter, you're just the man to feed my sheep. I don't want men who feel themselves superior, I want men who have had personal experience of me as their shepherd, and are prepared to mediate that to their brothers and sisters when they go astray. That's who I want.'

Even in the most intimate and exalted moments the Lord was ever a realist. There were lessons to teach Peter about not lording it over the flock. He said to him, '*Feed* my lambs and *tend* my sheep.'

That is how Peter was able to say in his first letter,

> So I exhort the elders among you, as a fellow elder and a witness of the sufferings of Christ, as well as a partaker in the glory that is going to be revealed: shepherd the flock of God that is among you, exercising oversight, not under compulsion, but willingly, as God would have you; not for shameful gain, but eagerly; not domineering over those in your charge, but being examples to the flock. And when the chief Shepherd appears, you will receive the unfading crown of glory.' (1 Pet 5:1–4)

This is something perhaps that will be better considered without a multiplicity of words from me. Rather, in the quiet of our hearts, let each of us say to the Lord, 'In my service for you, Lord, what is my motive? Do I love using the big stick and the rod, and fencing people in with walls, or have I learned the value that you place on an individual sheep because you did so much for me, one of the worst of your sheep? Lord, you know that I do love you, for I would have been lost without you, my testimony would have been ruined and I wouldn't have lasted five minutes. And because I've learned how valuable it is to have a shepherd who loves like that, and because I love my shepherd, I would count it a great privilege to be allowed in my turn to look after your sheep in the same fashion.'

The limits of a shepherd

There on the beach, Christ added, 'But before we finish, Peter, you need to learn that there are certain limits to your work. You may not be thinking of it now, but that day will come when you will have to lay it down. When you were young, you used to dress yourself and go wherever you wanted. You saw that there was a job to be done and you got up and did it. Wasn't that a lovely thing to be able to do? But when you are old, you will lose that power. Others will dress you and carry you where you do not want to go.'

Finishing well

Christ was still the shepherd, putting signposts along the journey so that his sheep wouldn't get worried and feel he had lost his way in the difficulties of old age. 'Peter,' he says, 'I want you to know that I have a service for you to do now when you are young, and I have a service for you when you are old and can no longer do what you formerly did.' In Peter's case it would be a question of persecution and imprisonment. His service would come to an abrupt end, which wasn't the kind of thing he'd choose. 'But Peter,' he says, 'I want you to know that you'll glorify me in that too.'

This should come as a comfort to Christian brothers and sisters who are growing older. Once you loved to be active in the Lord's work; you sought out the sheep, you did your visitation, you helped in numberless ways. When you saw a job to be done, you did it. You are growing older now, and you don't have the strength. You can't concentrate as you used to and read your Bible, and you can't get out to meet with the Lord's people as often as you would like to, and it seems a frustration. You begin to think, 'What use am I to the Lord?'

What use are you to the Lord! When you have done your little bit of shepherding, you are still his sheep. You are always valuable and your value will not decrease. He values you, not because of the work you did, but because of who you are. You are his sheep right to the very end, even all the way home to glory.

Can you still be a shepherd? You can glorify God by showing some of our youngsters the glory of a life that not only started well but ended well. It's easy when you have learned the theory to get up and speak, isn't it? It's quite another thing to have done fifty years on the road and then to go home triumphantly, glorifying God. That is the biggest test of all shepherds—the way they finish their journey.

Shepherding, not controlling

'But, Peter,' said Christ, 'I want you to remember that there are limits to your work even as a shepherd.'

Peter turned round and saw John following them, and he said, 'Lord, what about this man?'

The Lord said, 'What is that to you?'

That was blunt, wasn't it?

'What John does is nothing to do with you, Peter. That's my responsibility. If it is my will that he remain until I come, what is that to you? You follow me!' (see John 21:22). He wanted Peter to shepherd the sheep, but he didn't want Peter controlling the other servants, and the church would have done well to learn the lesson. The human heart is a curious thing. Sometimes we'd rather control the servant than look after the sheep. What great organizations the church has built for controlling servants.

So the Lord said, 'Please will you leave that thing to me, Peter?'

Peter did as he was told. You'll never read once in all the Acts of the Apostles that Peter attempted to tell another servant what to do. Some had a go at telling Peter, of course. When he preached the gospel to the Gentiles, they hauled him up and said, 'Give an account of this' (Acts 11). But you will never find Peter interfering, not even on that great occasion when Paul and Barnabas fell out and couldn't agree on methods in the Lord's work. You don't read that Peter stepped in and said, 'Look here, Barnabas, this won't do.' He hadn't authority to do anything; that was the Lord's business, and servants must be left free to be immediately responsible to their Lord.

That is important when thinking about the principles that guide the church. We've got enough to do without going outside our tasks. Shepherds must know what their tasks are, and what they are not. Let us remember, please, the sufferings of Christ. What did Christ die for? That he might forgive our sins, yes, but for another reason— he died 'that he might be Lord' (Rom 14:9), not you or me. The art of the shepherd is not to get between the sheep and the Lord. It is to bring the sheep to the Lord. It is far more important in daily life that believers make their own decisions before him. The valuable thing is in trying to please the Lord, and if the person we are concerned about is honestly trying to please him we can leave it there, and the Lord will guide. Let us learn our limitations, lest with very good desire we get between the sheep and the Lord, and the sheep merely do things because we say so, instead of their personal decision as free men and women before the Lord. It will take tremendous wisdom and grace for elders in particular to know where to draw the line.

These were the lessons that the Lord taught Peter after he had restored him and reappointed him to feed *his* sheep. 'Feed *my* sheep', he had said to Peter those three times. And, having been taught by the great shepherd through many years' experience, Peter says, 'As the Lord made himself an example to me, may God give you grace to make yourselves examples to the flock.'

Peter had been appointed to his task by the risen Lord, but it was his own experience of the Lord's loving care and restoration after dismal failure that prepared him, in his turn and for his time, to shepherd the Lord's people. He never forgot how the Lord had been his shepherd, and those who were in his care reaped the benefit.

From Willingness *to* Belief

Truly, truly, I say to you, whoever hears my word and believes him who sent me has eternal life. He does not come into judgement, but has passed from death to life. Truly, truly, I say to you, an hour is coming, and is now here, when the dead will hear the voice of the Son of God, and those who hear will live. For as the Father has life in himself, so he has granted the Son also to have life in himself. And he has given him authority to execute judgement, because he is the Son of Man.

John 5:24–27

Reading and believing

Perhaps it is clear enough by now what I meant at the beginning of this book when I said that John's Gospel is intended to lead us personally to faith in Christ. That much we can see from the stories we have considered. We have not, of course, considered them all. There are a great many more and, especially if you have never done so, I encourage you to continue reading the entire Gospel for yourself and listen as God speaks his living word to you.

But how shall we know that the Gospel of John really is the word of God? Well, at least one thing is certain—you should not wait until you know it's the word of God before you read it, or you'll be like the man who said he would never go into the water until he learned to swim! If you want to know that it is the word of God, read it carefully and patiently, allowing God to do his life-giving work in your heart.

We should remember as well that the Gospel of John comes to us with the authority of Jesus Christ. If what it says is true, here is God our Creator trying to communicate with us, trying to talk to us personally, trying to reveal himself to us, so that through Jesus Christ we may enter into a personal relationship of faith and love with him. Not to be interested in discovering whether it is true or not; not to be interested in the possibility of hearing our Creator speak to us, might seem to indicate a strange, irrational predisposition on our part.

Of course I am not asking you to believe it before you start reading it. But I am asking you to read it, and then make up your mind whether it's true or not. After all, that's how you treat the news, isn't it? You know before you start that some of the things your chosen news sources contain will be true, and some not. You certainly do not decide, before you read, to believe whatever they say. But that doesn't stop you reading them. You have confidence enough in your own judgment to read what they say, to reflect on it and to make up your own mind whether it's true or not. I'm asking you to do the same with the Gospel of John.

And if you do, Jesus Christ himself guarantees that, provided you are prepared to fulfil one condition, God will show you personally whether his claims are true or not. And the condition is this: 'If anyone is willing to do God's will'—that is, when he discovers what it is—'he will find out whether my teaching comes from God or whether I speak on my own' (John 7:17 own trans.). He will find out, because, as he reads and studies and thinks about what Jesus taught, God will speak to his heart, and show him beyond shadow of doubt that what Jesus says is true.

The trouble lies, I suspect, with the condition: 'If anyone is willing to do God's will'. We sense before we start, that if God did show us the truth, it would carry profound implications for our way of life that we might not wish to face. So we would prefer to approach the whole thing impersonally, like we approach experiments in physics, without committing ourselves in advance to any practical implications. But we cannot treat God like that. We cannot come to the Almighty and say: 'Yes, I would like to know whether you are there or not, and whether Jesus Christ is your Son or not. Please show me. But I would like you to understand that if you reveal yourself to me, I still am not necessarily prepared to do anything you might tell me to do.' God has no time for spiritual dilettantes.

But if you are serious, and willing to do God's will when you know it, then make the experiment. Read the Gospel of John seriously with an open mind, and Jesus Christ guarantees that God will show you what the truth is.

The story of the man who was born blind
Someone will be saying, perhaps, 'My trouble is this: I don't even know whether God exists. If I made the experiment you suggest, would I not be in danger of imagining I heard God speak to me, when it was only auto-suggestion? How would I recognize God, even if he did speak to me?'

Well, let me finish with one last story from John's Gospel. You can find it in chapter 9. It is about a miracle Jesus did when he came across a man who had been born blind, and asked him if he would like to be given sight.

I don't know if you have ever tried to explain to someone born blind what sight is, or what colour is like, or even to convince them that there are such things as light and colour, but it is mighty difficult! We could have well understood it, therefore, if the blind man had replied to Jesus, that he didn't know what sight was, and considered all claims that there was such a thing as sight to be nonsense. That, at least, is how many people react these days when they hear Jesus

Christ say that he can give them spiritual sight; that he can give them eternal life, which is the faculty of knowing God personally (17:3).

Fortunately, however, the blind man said that if there was such a thing as sight he would like to have it. So Jesus Christ suggested to the man that there was an experiment he could perform, if he was willing to; and he guaranteed that if he performed it, he would receive sight.

Now the experiment Christ laid down seemed a strange experiment, as you will discover if you read the story. But the blind man was not one who was deliberately opposed to discovering the truth. He reasoned that Jesus Christ was no charlatan, nor lunatic either. If he said there was a thing called sight and that he could give it to anyone who wanted it, then it was worth making the experiment. There was nothing to lose. There was everything to gain. So he made the experiment, found by personal experience that it worked, and returned from the experiment seeing.

I recommend a similar experiment to you. Read John's Gospel. As you read, say: 'God, I'm not sure if you exist. But if you do, and if Jesus is your Son and he can give me, as he claims, eternal life, whatever that is, speak to me, reveal yourself to me, show me that Jesus is your Son. And if you show me, I am prepared to do your will, whatever it turns out to be.'

And Christ guarantees that God will show you.

Scripture Index

Scripture Index

Scripture Index

Other Resources on John's Gospel

At the time of publication of this volume, two further books on the Gospel of John are in production. The first is a larger book that will present David Gooding's extensive teaching on this Gospel as fully as possible. The second is an overview of the Gospel designed to equip Bible teachers and students of God's word.

The resources listed below are free for you to read and/or listen to on our website (myrtlefieldhouse.com). New resources continue to be added as they become available to us. To stay up to date with these, join our email newsletter.

Myrtlefield Expositions

In the School of Christ
Lessons on Holiness in John 13–17

Myrtlefield Sermons

The Upper Room Ministry
Twelve Conversational Studies on John 13–17

On the Road with Jesus
Fifteen Studies on Major Themes in John's Gospel

Four Journeys to Jerusalem
Nineteen Studies on Major Themes in John's Gospel

When I Go Away
One Study on the Lord's Provision in John 14

Knowledge of the Living Lord
Five Studies on Select Themes from John's Gospel

The Fight for Our Sanctification
Four Studies on Christ's Work from John 13–16

The Fourth Journey to Jerusalem
Four Studies on John 11–12 and 18–19

Structure and Meaning
Two Studies Providing a Literary Analysis of John's Gospel

The School of Holiness
Four Studies on Sanctification from John 13–16

Highway to Holiness
Fifteen Studies on Major Themes in John 13–16

The Gleam of Eternal Glory
Two Studies on Select Passages in John

www.myrtlefieldhouse.com

Our website contains hundreds of resources in a variety of formats. You can read, listen to or watch David Gooding's teaching on over 35 Bible books and 14 topics. You can also view the full catalogue of Myrtlefield House publications and download free e-book editions of most of our books and all of our sermon transcripts. The website is optimized for both computer and mobile viewing, making it easy for you to access the resources at home or on the go.

For more information about any of our publications or resources contact us at: info@myrtlefieldhouse.com

Myrtlefield Expositions

Myrtlefield Expositions provide insights into the thought flow and meaning of the biblical writings, motivated by devotion to the Lord who reveals himself in the Scriptures. Scholarly, engaging, and accessible, each book addresses the reader's mind and heart to increase faith in God and to encourage obedience to his word. Teachers, preachers and all students of the Bible will find the approach to Scripture adopted in these volumes both instructive and enriching.

The Riches of Divine Wisdom
The New Testament's Use of the Old Testament

According to Luke
The Third Gospel's Ordered Historical Narrative

True to the Faith
The Acts of the Apostles: Defining and Defending the Gospel

In the School of Christ
Lessons on Holiness in John 13–17

An Unshakeable Kingdom
The Letter to the Hebrews for Today

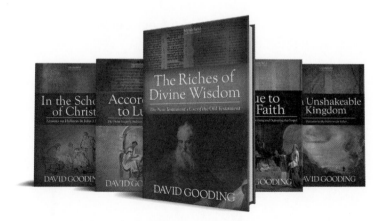

Myrtlefield Encounters

Myrtlefield Encounters are complementary studies of biblical literature, Christian teaching and apologetics. The books in this series engage the minds of believers and sceptics. They show how God has spoken in the Bible to address the realities of life and its questions, problems, beauty and potential.

Key Bible Concepts
Defining the Basic Terms of the Christian Faith

Christianity: Opium or Truth?
Answering Thoughtful Objections to the Christian Faith

The Definition of Christianity
Exploring the Original Meaning of the Christian Faith

The Bible and Ethics
Finding the Moral Foundations of the Christian Faith

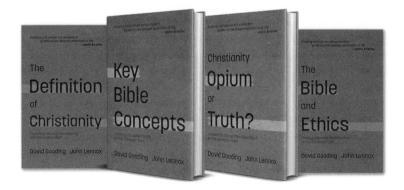

Our lives are a mix of difficulties, laughter and delight, of satisfying moments, seemingly hopeless situations and unanswerable questions. Nature's beauty inspires our wonder today, but its power may break our bodies tomorrow. What will steady our faith in God, and help it to grow, when life is like that?

Far from wanting us to live in a make-believe world, the call of God's word is to see the reality of what God is doing in the lives of millions of people. Scripture tells us that, right now, he is working out his long-term plan for bringing many sons and daughters to full maturity in his Son, Jesus Christ. The more we understand the revelation of his plan, and the character of the one who has decided to bring us on a journey through this world of brokenness and beauty, the more we will be drawn to follow him in obedience, love and trust.

These 365 one-page readings focus on Christ's work as the captain of our salvation, on the way he journeys with his redeemed, and finally on the wisdom and love of the Father who planned it all.

You will consider *Bringing Us To Glory* one of God's best gifts to your own devotional life. Read it, and reap! — *O. S. Hawkins*

This book is equal to a full year at any theological college. I realize more than ever why so many of my friends have been mentored by Dr Gooding. — *George Verwer*

It is clear we are reading a man who has fallen in love with the glory and majesty of God. This is a must read! — *Rebecca Manley Pippert*

7th February

CHRIST THE MEANS OF LIFE

Reading: John 6:1–15

This was to fulfil the word that he had spoken: 'Of those whom you gave me I have lost not one.' (John 18:9)

Consider what the bread is. It is not only 'the bread of life' it is 'the *living* bread'. The manna came down from heaven, but it wasn't alive itself! Our Lord is the living bread. This bread is alive. When the miracle of the feeding of the five thousand took place, we are told that, after the crowds had eaten and were filled, our Lord instructed the apostles to go around and gather up the broken pieces of the bread that remained so 'that nothing may be lost' (6:12). That is an interesting remark. We might say, 'But if our Lord had the power to multiply loaves and fishes to feed five thousand, what does it matter if a few broken pieces were left lying around and left to rot? He could easily make some more, couldn't he?' But he gave them instructions, and they had to gather up the broken pieces that remained so that nothing of that bread would be lost.

How much more the people he has saved. You claim that Christ saved you and is your bread of life, and he is in you? Well, I can tell you now that that bread shall *never* be lost. 'Christ in you'—the living bread. It is a magnificent concept, but an even more magnificent reality: Christ has come to live *in* us!

We have to be prepared for life in a spirit world. Our Lord's resurrection body is said to be a 'spiritual body'. That doesn't mean, as some people say, that our resurrection body is made of spirit and is not genuinely material, any more than if I told you that this man's car has a petrol engine you would imagine that the engine is made of petrol. Petrol is the stuff that makes it go as distinct from a diesel engine or an electric motor.

So too with the resurrection body of Christ. He said, 'Touch me, and see. For a spirit does not have flesh and bones as you see that I have' (Luke 24:39). It was a real and, in our sense, a physical body, but of a different order. It is a *spiritual body*. If you are Christ's, you have within you that very power that shall raise you at the resurrection when the Lord comes (if you have to be raised), or shall transform you when you meet the Lord in the air.

Myrtlefield Discoveries

Myrtlefield Discoveries combine depth of insight with accessible style in order to help today's readers find the Bible's meaning and its significance for all of life. Covering whole books of the Bible, themes or topics, each book in this series serves as a guide to the wonders of God's word. The material is intended to prepare readers to share what they have learned. Study groups, teachers and individual students will all benefit from the way these books open up the biblical text and reveal its application for life.

Windows on Paradise
Scenes of Hope and Salvation in the Gospel of Luke

Journeys with Jesus
True Stories of Changed Destinies in John's Gospel

Drawing Near To God
Lessons From the Tabernacle for Today

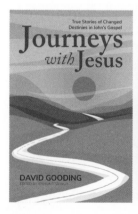
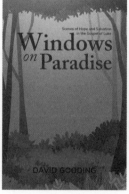
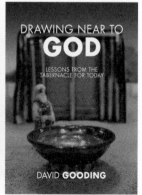